The Bible of Investing 2021

Amazon fba, dropshipping, affiliate
marketing, stock trading, house
flipping and much more. the definitive
guide to achieve super performance
after the pandemic

4 BOOKS IN 1

Make Money Online After the Pandemic

Proven methods to Achieve Super Performance in 2021 | Definitive Guide to Generate More Than $10,000/Month

BOOK 1

Table of Contents

Intoduction

The Internet has revolutionized the way we work. Workplaces and jobs are not what they used to be. Long gone are the days when everything was done by humans and paper was the only way to communicate. The truth is that the digital economy is booming. In the next few years, you will most likely be self-employed, making a living online or running your own business online or working for someone else who runs their business entirely or mostly online.

We're entering the age of the Internet of Things where almost everything will be connected online: from street dumpsters that will alert authorities when they need to be emptied, to wearable devices and smart clothing that will tell you when it's best for you to eat and when you're most productive. For this book, we've broken down the various ways to make money online into 5 main categories:

1. DIGITAL WORKING

2. RESIDUAL INCOME (SEMI-PASSIVE)

3. ONLINEBUSINESS (ENTREPRENEUR)

4. INVEST ONLINE

5. SELL OR RENT WHAT YOU HAVE OR WHAT YOU DO

Whichever way you choose to begin this journey is based on what you want to achieve, what risk you are willing to take, how much time you have, how much money you may already have, and what kind of income you want to make.

NOTE: This ebook was created to give advice and concrete possibilities of gain to all people who are living with suffering the period related to the global pandemic. Choosing some of the earning methods within the guide you will not become rich in most cases, but you will be able to get a good income to live with carefree even the darkest periods.

I have avoided inserting Links while reading. You can find everything you need in the USEFUL LINKS section at the end of the ebook.

Chapter 1:

LET'S LOOK AT THE DIFFERENT WAYS TO MAKE MONEY ONLINE

Digital work is low-risk since you're essentially taking on a job that pays you for your time or output. However, it also has few advantages as most digital employees don't do much, compared to the other riskier options. To work in digital, you don't need to have any specific knowledge, but for some of the other methods we'll discuss in this section, having an area of expertise, such as writing, is essential.

This option is low-risk as it requires no upfront investment, as most of the sites we've mentioned below have no commissions. Digital work includes things like freelancing, music review, writing, consulting, translating, displaying advertisements, and more.

Residual (semi-passive) income opportunities on the other hand can be medium to low risk depending on whether you are investing only your time, or time and money, in creating the resources necessary to eventually produce semi-passive residual income. You may not find the formula that works for you the first or second time around, but the rewards can really be life-changing if you do things right.

We prefer the term "residual income" over "passive income" which is commonly referred to online, as "passive" implies that you don't have to do anything once you have something working, but that's usually not the case. In this section we'll cover methods like affiliate marketing. The creative among us may want to try writing and selling e-books, creating a YouTube channel, creating apps, podcasts, or stock content (photos, videos, music/audio).

Online business (entrepreneur) is a section dedicated to entrepreneurial personalities. We cover things like starting your own business when you don't have much experience in the industry or service you provide, and how to take advantage of the knowledge or passion you have and make a profit. We include ecommerce ideas like dropshipping, web design, web or app development, I.T. support business and many more.

These options are quite risky as they require an initial investment and much more time than the methods mentioned above. However, one of the main positives is that you can work from home while doing so - and you are effectively your own boss. The idea behind this is that you are in charge of the business and outsource work to professionals when necessary. This type of online business approach works best for handymen; people who can do accounting, marketing, and human resources.

Investing online doesn't mean you have to have a lot of savings. You can get started with as little as $50. This option will require you to do research before putting down your money. Most of these investments are entirely based on research, information, and accurate predictions, which means that if you think of yourself as someone unlucky, you can catch a break. We include investment methods such as matched betting, stock trading, forex trading and more. The level of risk depends on how much you're willing to invest.

There are no high rewards without high risks. In this section, we explain the different approaches to online investing, so that whether you are hesitant to risk large sums of money or enjoy the adrenaline rush of taking risks, we will help you choose the best methods for you and your needs.

Selling or renting what you have or do is exactly what it sounds like. We all have space we don't use or, if you're a hoarder, the exact opposite: an excess of stuff. In this section, we talk about how you can make money from what you have like appliances, furniture or old clothes and what you can make and sell, like knitted sweaters or custom artwork. We will also discuss how and what you can rent to people . This could include things like your home for filming, spare rooms for tenants, parking spaces, storage or other assets. There is a level of risk associated with this option, however, as you may experience damage to your rented items or the items you sold may want to be returned, which creates additional shipping costs.

Chapter 2:

DIGITAL WORKING

Getting paid to do a job online (trading your time for money like any normal job).

Risk Factor: **LOW**

Reward Factor: **LOW**

The following 16 ways to make money online in this section are for those people who do not like risks and simply want to get paid for their time like any normal job. There are many ways to earn money online for your time and the best one for you will depend on your current skills or the ones you are willing to learn.

Digital work can offer enormous life freedoms such as the freedom to work the hours you want, the freedom to work wherever you are or want to live, and the freedom to choose who you work for.

Digital work can also offer some drawbacks compared to a conventional job such as the risk of not getting paid on time or at all (be careful to check with employers), the risk of losing your job on very short notice, and the risk of loosening periods without any work.

The secret to success with digital work is to be good at what you do. Choose something you're experienced or passionate about to learn and master the work you do. That way you can command higher rates per hour (or per job) and you'll always be in demand. There are some online jobs that don't require as much expertise and generally pay less.

Number 1: FREELANCE

Freelance services on sites such as: upwork.com - fiverr.com - guru.com freelancer.com - peopleperhour.com - microworkers.com or similar.

A freelancer is an individual who offers different types of online work for an employer or company. They are usually not engaged with one employer.

Freelancers can switch between jobs or hold multiple jobs at once. They can be short term or long term. Freelancing is a popular way to make money online and it is also one of the easiest ways to get a job. There are many places online where you can start working as a freelancer. Some of the most popular websites are:

- upwork.com
- fiverr.com
- guru.com
- freelancer.com
- peopleperhour.com
- microworkers.com

Registering on a website like freelancer.com is generally free; but some sites also offer paid packages or subscriptions that give the freelancer more visibility.

Doing freelance work gives you the advantage of working in the comfort of your own home and working at your own pace. Getting paid is also relatively quick for this type of work as well. You can receive payments through online money transfer services like PayPal or TransferWise (directly into your bank account).

On the other hand, freelancing can also be a risky business. You could be unknowingly working for scammers, which is why you need to do extensive research on your clients and be very careful about who you work for. Working on reputable sites like the ones mentioned above is also a way to protect yourself. One of the most reliable freelance sources online is Freelancer.

Number 2: VIRTUAL ASSISTANT

Work as a full-time or part-time virtual employee, usually for foreign employers, through sites like onlinejobs.ph or virtualemployee.com.

A virtual employee or Virtual Assistant (VA) is a self-employed person who offers services over the Internet. They usually focus on providing technical, administrative, social, or creative assistance to their distant employers. Often these online workers perform multiple tasks for one employer, but you may choose to have many employers for whom you perform part-time administrative tasks.

Working as a virtual employee brings many benefits to the worker. For some, they can work at their leisure, whenever they wish as long as they perform tasks or hours each week. While for others, they may be required to work with online supervision. Sometimes virtual assistants are required during the employer's working hours, which could mean night work if the employer is on the other side of the world. They may be required to be online even when their employer is there. But it depends on what they agreed to when they were hired.

Being a virtual assistant also means flexibility to do different types of tasks. Some employers require someone who is skilled in everything they need help with. But there are also employers who are willing to train their virtual assistant to do some tasks they've never done before.

Working from the comfort of home is always the biggest perk of being a virtual assistant or VA. But just like any other online job, it can be risky. That's why it's best to make sure you don't fall into the hands of a bad employer. Some of the best online places for VA jobs can be found at www.onlinejobs.ph or www.virtualemployee.com.

Number 3: PAYING SURVEYS AND MARKET RESEARCH

Paid surveys and research on sites such as swagbucks.com - i-say.com - mysurvey.com - cashcrate.com or similar.

With websites like swagbucks.com, i-say.com, mysurvey.com and cashcrate.com you can get paid or rewarded for reading, watching and shopping online.

Earning money through paid surveys is a very convenient way to earn money online. All you have to do is register for a profile and start taking surveys. Registration is free, easy and fast.

Some paid survey websites like swagbucks.com offer many options for earning money. They often give out gift certificates for each task completed. They also give you the convenience of choosing from options such as taking surveys, watching videos, or shopping online through their website.

While paid surveys and research can be an easy way to make some extra money online, they can also be risky as there are many "paid survey" scam websites online, so be careful.

Most of these scam websites require you to pay a registration fee or upgrade your subscription, so avoid such sites. Others may not ask you for commissions but pay you almost nothing or nothing at all. So before doing paid surveys and research for anyone, make sure you double check their legitimacy first.

Number 4: ANSWER TO QUESTIONS AND TIPS

Answering questions and giving advice on sites such as kgb.com, justanswer.com, webanswers.com or similar.

Whether you are a consultant or not, answering questions and giving advice might be perfect for you if you have good or expert knowledge on any subject. This type of work works best for those who are verified and licensed professionals - those who are experts at what they do.

All over the world, people are looking for answers to questions they can't answer or things they simply can't figure out how to do. That's why websites like kgb.com, justanswer.com and other similar places online have been created.

If you are a doctor, a lawyer, a mechanic or an expert in anything you do, this way to make money is for you. Websites created to answer people's questions are not free. Once a person accesses the website and asks an expert, they are more than willing to pay the price to get an answer right away. In return, you give them what they need by answering their question until they are completely satisfied. This saves your time and makes you some extra money at the same time.

Answering questions and giving advice can be an easy way to generate extra income online. The pay is fair and the efforts are generally low. On the other hand, when there is dissatisfaction with your answer, you may not get paid. This can be demotivating, as you have potentially wasted your time and efforts only to end up with nothing if your answers and advice are not considered good or helpful.

Number 5: COPYWRITING

There is a huge demand for copywriters to write copy for websites, blogs, social media, articles, e-books, advertisements etc.

Copywriting is the term used to describe written content in print materials and online media. Copywriters produce articles that are used for slogans, emails, web content, sales channels and press releases to name a few. The copy must be 100% original and well-written; engaging, interesting and timely.

One of the most in-demand online employees are copywriters. Businesses all over the world, big or small, need creative marketing to increase their exposure. Copywriters can be paid by the hour or by project depending on the agreement made with their client.

The best thing about copywriting is that you can get your creativity flowing with words. This is a fun job for those who are passionate about writing. Usually the writing is done unsupervised, which can be very unhelpful for writers as without clear guidelines, you may have to resubmit the work many times before it is approved. Most projects have strict deadlines depending on the nature of the business or the marketing goals of the client.

Number 6: BLOGGING FOR OTHER PEOPLE'S WEBSITES

Blog websites are extremely common and popular, but often blog owners don't write, so there are opportunities to get paid to write blog posts for others.

Blogging is a great way to promote yourself, build an affiliate marketing business or promote your company's services/products in the digital world. Blogs are a great source of information for their readers and an engaging blog can get you a loyal following from users.

Not all blogs contain writings by the person who owns them. They are often written by someone who writes blogs for a living, commonly known as a "blogger." Many freelancers are paid to do blogs for other people's websites. When a project is underway, they may be paid by the hour, but they are usually paid a set amount per blog post written (usually about 500-750 words).

Some set a low price when there is a large number of rewrites, while others keep their rates high especially if they are professional writers in technical fields. Expertise in a particular area allows you to increase your rates.

Writing blogs may seem simple when you read them, but the truth is that good blogs are well researched and well polished articles. If writing original content is something you are capable of doing, blogging might be perfect for you. Some bloggers are happy to just write for other people, as they get a fair payment for their work. However, other bloggers prefer to produce work for their own brand or blogging website. Often, a blogger is not credited unless they are recognized as an official writer or staff of the company or client.

Number 7: GHOSTWRITING

A ghostwriter is that professional who is commissioned to write a book, eBook, white paper, or article on a topic for someone who is usually already fairly well known but doesn't have the time or skills to write what they need.

Ghost-writing is a term used for books, articles, stories and other texts that are written by another author without giving them official credit. In the corporate world, celebrities such as celebrities, political leaders and executives hire ghost writers to write or proofread and edit written materials that aim to promote them. The same goes for most companies that hire freelancers, as they usually do not credit them.

Making money with ghostwriting is as easy as blogging. However, ghostwriting requires more effort, attention to detail and is a much longer process. The way ghostwriters get paid depends on the type of writing they are assigned to. Contract signatures are required in most ghostwriting projects to ensure privacy and protection of the company's rights. Depending on the company's agreement with their ghost writers, they may be paid in full before the project begins, gradually, or upon completion.

However, ghostwriters are most likely reluctant to sign a contract where payments are made only upon completion of the project. Ghost-writing is a great way to improve your writing skills without the pressure of suffering criticism of your writing. However, it also takes away your exposure and right to own the content you've produced.

Number 8: SEO SERVICES

SEO or search engine optimization is the process of helping a website achieve higher organic search results in search engines like Google.

In digital marketing, SEO is a strategy to attract more visitors to a business website in hopes that they can be converted into customers. SEO helps improve a website's organic search engine rankings through keywords and phrases that people use to do a search.

You need to have a very good understanding of the many elements that make up SEO and will best optimize a website for search engines and the end user. Businesses or online clients constantly need someone to perform SEO services for them and usually pay more than they would for writers. This type of online work is usually paid gradually depending on the agreed upon setup. Rates can vary and can be hourly or per website.

The good thing about making money through SEO services is that there is a lot of demand for this kind of work. Also, you don't have to work for one company because it's not a daily task. However, it is an ongoing job - very technical and it has to be done well; otherwise, you will spend a lot of time tweaking your work when things go wrong. Normally, clients might abandon you quickly if your work does not get positive results for their website.

Number 9: TRANSLATION SERVICES

As the Internet makes it easier for companies to sell to a global audience, they are increasingly looking to provide their website content in multiple languages.

Translation is the process in which a language or text is communicated into another language through its meaning. It allows two or more people to understand each other despite their language barrier. The process of translation can take place in different ways such as word for word, sentence for sentence, etc. So, if you are fluent in more than one language, providing translation services could offer good online job opportunities for you.

Communication has become much easier since the rise of online translation services. Modern technology makes it convenient to find someone who can do it for you. Businesses, website owners or even college students are looking for someone to translate their text, website content, audio or conversations into another language. Some of these clients visit independent websites to look for the right translator. You can get paid as quickly as you do your job, to the standard you want.

Providing translation services allows you to benefit from a couple of advantages. You can work whenever you want. You can get paid as soon as you do your work or after the task is completed, depending on the agreement. There will be instances when you have to meet the deadline you have been given.

Number 10: WEBSITE USER INTERFACE TESTS

Website user interface (UI) testing with usertesting.com, trymyui.com or similar.

As you should know, a website is a place on the Internet that contains one or more pages of information about a person, company, product or service etc. The user interface is the design that focuses on giving users a great experience while they visit the site. Websites with a good user interface allow visitors to explore the pages and the information they contain and can generate calls to action and conversions (such as sales on an e-commerce website). Good user interface design does not draw attention to unnecessary details.

User interface testing not only applies to websites, but is also used for software development and mobile applications (Apps). Before launching a major website, app or product, designers and developers would often like to see firsthand what potential users think so they can iron out any numbers before they are launched and make overall improvements.

Such sites allow you to go through testing phases of the website user interface like usertesting.com, trymyui.com and other similar online places. They need people like you, who are potential users to try out the website or app and provide them with honest and helpful reviews. Every review or feedback makes you money as the owners improve their products which will also make more money later on.

Website UI testing is a great way to make money online. It's affordable, it's easy to do, and it allows you to help produce better products that you might even benefit from later on. The only thing you need to make sure of is to give them your best and honest review and make yourself available for testing.

Number 11: COMPLETE SMALL TASKS

Completing small tasks with clickworker.com, microworkers.com, Amazon's mturk.com or similar.

Jobs are jobs, no matter how big or small. And for every job, there is normally a contractor and an employee. Completing small tasks has become one of the trends in the online world today. These jobs can be called micro-jobs because of how short and simple they are. They can be repetitive tasks or a big task broken down into smaller parts.

Completing small tasks is easy. They include things like copywriting, proofreading, and web research. Websites like clickworker.com, microworkers.com, Amazon's mturk.com offer you these types of opportunities. Small tasks don't pay as much as other freelance or online jobs because they are micro-jobs. Some of these types of tasks pay pennies per task, but they are also very easy and quick to do.

It also allows you to do several jobs at once and as many as possible. If you are fast enough, you can do enough jobs to get to a decent amount. There is no limit to the number of jobs that you can do and most of them are at your convenience.

Number 12: LOOKING AT ONLINE ADVERTISEMENTS

Look at online ads with perk.com or similar.

An ad is a public advertisement that promotes a product, event or service. Online ads are messages we see on Web pages and videos on the Internet. Just like any advertising communication, their purpose is promotion. While watching a video you've probably come across an ad and wanted to click "x" or "close" immediately. This is common in YouTube videos where they can appear halfway through watching a video.

To help ad owners generate revenue, websites like perk.com have been created as a way to display their ads. In return, anyone who views such ads through their website gets points that they can later exchange for cash, gift certificates and prizes. Viewing online ads on perk.com allows you to get rewards every time you view one. So, it's like making money while having fun. It's fast, fun and easy.

While the convenience of watching online ads is incomparable to any other source of online income, the rewards and points you get are not that much so you will have to watch a lot of ads to earn decent cash rewards.

Number 13: REVISING MUSIC

Review music for money on sites like slicethepie.com or similar.

Artists, creators, and marketers have always loved getting feedback. It's a way to help them improve their craft and see if it's what people are looking for or not. This is why feedback, or more commonly known as a "review," is important for anyone who wants to get their music out into the online world.

One of the best places to make money online by reviewing music is at slicethepie.com. At SliceThePie.com, you give your detailed opinion about the music you hear on their website. You can give as many reviews as you want. Before the music is released, you have the luxury of being able to listen to them and give your feedback. In return, you get paid.

Getting paid by doing reviews is a very simple task. However, you have a responsibility to create a quality review for every piece of music you come across. Your income depends on the type of reviews you give to each creator. On SliceThePie.com, the higher your star rating and the quality of your reviews, the more you will get paid. If you work hard enough and take this online source of income seriously, your income will continue to grow.

Chapter 3:

RESIDUAL INCOME (SEMI-PASSIVE)

C reating sites and/or resources with the goal of creating residual (ongoing) revenue streams, getting paid again and again after all the initial work is completed

Risk factor: **MEDIUM-LOW**
Reward Factor: **LOW-HIGH**

The following 15 ways to make money online in this section are for those who are ready to build valuable websites or businesses while not getting paid for as long as it takes to produce them, but can earn a good residual monthly income over time. With these types of income, you can usually do something once and then earn money again and again for years.

Residual (semi-passive) income can offer tremendous life freedoms such as the freedom to live anywhere, buy some of the finer things in life, work as much or as little as you want, and spend more time with your family and friends.

Residual income can be hard to come by and will usually take a lot of initial time (no money), some financial outlay (to build and promote resources) and quite often will involve one or two failures along the way as you learn more about what works and what doesn't.

The secret to earning a residual (semi-passive) income is focus, commitment to massive initial work and persistence. It is advisable to choose to do something you are interested in or ideally have a passion for. It will also make the journey more enjoyable for you and help you commit to the goal in the first few months when you're training to try to get things right.

Number 14: AFFILIATE MARKETING - INDEPENDENT SALES

Creating small websites or social media channels that promote other people's products that you don't use or have an interest in (affiliate marketing). Affiliate marketing is the term used to sell or promote other people's products online. In the offline world, it is commonly known as reselling.

Making money through affiliate marketing requires a lot of work, especially in the beginning. If you're a beginner, you can start by finding other people's products that you want to promote. You can do this by searching for "affiliate program" or "partner program" on search engines like Google, or by searching for a company's affiliate program like "Virgin Affiliate Program". You can also use websites like cj.com, clickbank.com and affiliateprograms.com to more easily find a range of companies and products with affiliate programs.

On those websites, you'll see an extensive list of products and retailers that you can choose from. While it's best to try and choose something that interests you, many affiliate retailers simply choose whatever they feel they can make money from promoting.

This is called independent selling. Since you will have to promote products through websites and social media channels that you create, if you have a passion for what you are promoting, your job will be much easier and more enjoyable as we will see in the next example.

After choosing a product or products you want to promote from those that pay a decent commission on all the sales you can make from sending customers to the retailers website, you then need to start promoting them. This step takes a lot of time up front and works either by building websites or social media pages like on Facebook, writing content (or outsourcing the writing work to others and paying them) and paying to boost posts or push ads to try and build a steady stream of visitors to your website or social page.

Number 15: AFFILIATE MARKETING - PERSONAL INTEREST

Creating and managing a blog website on a niche topic of personal interest and that you are passionate about, with affiliate links to recommended products (affiliate marketing).

Blogs can be about anything. They can be about your company, yourself, or your favorite product. Creating and writing a blog means writing engaging content that will entice people to want to read and continue reading whatever new content you write about. In a blog, you can express your opinions on anything you want to share. And for affiliates, it's a great way to make money by writing about a (niche) topic they're interested in, knowledgeable about, or passionate about.

You can write blogs about the products you use without sounding like a salesperson. Beauty bloggers can simply show a picture of the beauty products they use, write about why they use them, the benefits of the products and comparisons to other products, then provide a link to buy it online from another website they are affiliated with. And when they do, they drive traffic, make money and receive a sales commission from the retailer in exchange for the referral.

Creating and writing a blog for affiliate marketing is easy when you know the right steps to do it. However, you need to create a large enough following to start making money. This can take some time, but when you achieve it, it will pay off big time.

Number 16: SITE ADS

Make money with small ads on your website/blog.

If you have a blog or website that is already getting a decent number of visitors, why not try online advertising? It's a great way to leverage your audience and monetize your site. There are many free resources on the Internet that are entirely funded by advertising, make no mistake, it can be a great deal!

Well, the truth of the matter is that you have to have a considerable number of visitors visiting your site every day to make real money. There are two main ways to manage advertisers on your website. Firstly, you can manage it all by yourself. You can set up your own charges and try to attract advertisers; for some companies this proves to be the most profitable method. This method, by which you are actually selling your ad space, is often called "direct banner advertising" and allows you to determine your own rates.

However, an easier method is to use Google AdSense. Google tracks you on almost every website you visit, so it knows what you like the moment you click on certain ads and can direct them to you when you visit other websites that show ads. The downside of Google AdSense is that you don't choose the ads that appear on your website, Google does. It also shows different ads to different people, so it's very difficult to see which ads are showing on your website.

Simply sign up for a Google AdSense account, choose the size/format you want your ad to have, display the text and/or image, and copy and paste the code snippet into the space on the website you want your ad to appear on!

Number 17: ONLINE COURSE CREATION

Create online courses for Udemy.com, Teachable.com or similar.

Many people may have a skill or subject expertise that they could teach, but not everyone is given the opportunity to do so. Luckily, there are places like Udemy where you can monetize your expertise through the creation of online courses. Udemy is an online platform for experts and instructors to teach or anyone who wants to learn a particular subject.

They have a free course design tool that allows you to focus on what matters most: the content. Plus, with Udemy's 11 million learners, you can easily reach millions of learners around the world in the largest online learning marketplace.
Creating online courses for Udemy is easy when you know what you're teaching. You can start making money as soon as you're ready to create a course for your students. Creating courses on Udemy allows you to create 1-3 hours of content in both text and video formats.

There are 3 main ways to receive payments from Udemy:

"Instructor Promotion" is when you get 97% of the revenue by promoting and bringing new students to your course on their website. This has a 3% administrative fee. Udemy takes care of all the customer service, payment processing, hosting fees and everything else.

"Udemy Organic", is when you get a 50% revenue sharing fee on organic Udemy sales where no instructor coupons are used.

"Paid user acquisition channel sales," in most cases, are achieved when you reach 25% revenue sharing from the instructor. To optimize your sales, Udemy partners with affiliates through their global networks or pays for advertising your course.

To put it bluntly, there is significant money to be made using this site. Not only is it a simple and easy way to provide extra income, but it can help you build your own personal brand while making a real difference in the lives of students around the world.

Number 18: CREATING DIGITAL PRODUCTS

Create digital products to sell through ClickBank.com or similar.

Digital products are created electronically and are viewable and work only on devices such as smartphones, tablets, laptops or computers. When you purchase a digital product, it will be delivered to you via email attachment or via a download link.

Some of the most common digital products sold on ClickBank are short training courses, but software and apps are also common digital products sold on other platforms. Creating digital products to sell can be a great source of income as other people (affiliates) will be motivated to make the sale for you in exchange for a healthy affiliate commission (usually 50%).

If you want to make money online using these products, but don't have the skills to create them, a place like ClickBank would be a good place to start. They open you up to an extensive list of digital products that you can sell. You can use your own website or blog to start promoting the product. You can also simply use the product link that takes people to the sales page to start promoting them, even if you don't have a website.

Digital products are in high demand. They are usually cheap to buy and very convenient to sell because you don't need a physical store to showcase them and you don't have to ship any physical products via courier. It's like being able to carry your store inside your computer wherever you go. Creating great digital products that will sell well takes a lot of time and effort, but if done right they become a fantastic source of residual income for years to come after the initial effort.

Number 19: AFFILIATE MARKETING - AMAZON ASSOCIATE SHOP

Creating an Amazon Associates store (affiliate marketing). Amazon is one of the largest online stores in the world and currently operates in about 15 countries. With its huge product directory, easy-to-use interface, hassle-free payment methods, and quick delivery options, it's easy for most people to "go to" the site when it comes to buying online. Whatever you're looking to purchase, Amazon usually has it on sale.

Amazon also has an affiliate program called "Amazon Associates" that allows anyone who signs up for the program to promote Amazon products and earn a sales commission (up to 10%). If you already have a website and promote Amazon products through the program, every time someone chooses to click on the Amazon affiliate link and purchase products from Amazon, you earn a "referral" commission.

With Amazon Associates, you can also create your own online store that they call aStore. It allows you to feature Amazon products that you can embed or link to from your website or blog. In addition, you can also add a page on your website that showcases the aStore and customize it so that its appearance matches your website. For example, if you were running a fitness blog, aStore would be a perfect and easy way to display your favorite/recommended fitness equipment and products from Amazon on your site. Having aStore on your website gives your audience the convenience of shopping on the same page, while the Amazon logo and reliable shopping cart will prove the legitimacy of your store.

Setting up an Amazon Associates store is free and very simple. You can get started by joining their program and going directly to the aStore section of Associates central. It's quick to create your own aStore and no programming skills are required to do so. If aStore is not available in your country, another option is to create a WordPress website and populate that site with products from Amazon that are automatically placed on your website using a plug-in developed by WooZone.

Number 20: EBOOK

Possibility of residual income from writing ebooks.

An eBook is simply an electronic version of a book that can be read on all types of digital devices such as phones, tablets (like Kindles) and computers. Making money online through creating and selling eBooks requires a lot of initial work but little risk or cost. Also, becoming a self-published author is now easier than ever. This can largely be attributed to the sheer amount of companies offering their platform to help you get your content out into the world.

Unlike traditional publishing, there are minimal, if any, upfront costs - the biggest risk is simply time. Amazon's Amazon Direct Publishing (KDP) platform is one of the largest eBook platforms in the world. Not only is it fast, easy, and free, but it also offers generous royalties of up to 70%, compared to traditional publishing rates that usually range between 6% and 25%. In other words, companies like Amazon's KDP have now made it easy to become a self-published author and accessible to anyone.

When it comes to monetizing your eBook, there are a few ways you can do it. The quickest and easiest way to monetize your eBook is to simply sell it for a fixed price on Amazon's Kindle marketplace. Kindle has countless readers who are always looking for new publications. If your book offers them the kind of entertainment they are looking for, you can start making money right away.

Another option is to give your eBook away for free as an incentive. Perhaps your eBook is aimed at a niche or target audience? By making your eBook accessible for free in exchange for something like an email address, you can reach a much larger potential customer pool. Many people feel hesitant to purchase promotional products and courses online because of the lack of credibility and legitimacy online. Therefore, by providing them with free, valuable content, you're building trust, legitimacy, and authority with your audience.

In addition, some choose to place relevant promotional links (be it their own or affiliated products and courses) within their eBook. This is another easy way to maximize your eBook earnings.

Creating eBooks for Kindle is a simple process. It's a plus if you know how to organize ideas that could be turned into a book. But if writing is not your forte, you can also hire freelancers who can write for you. Even content for e-books needs to be well-researched and perfectly written. The same pressure you get from perfecting a physical book also applies when creating eBooks.

Number 21: YOUTUBE CHANNEL

YouTube channel (advertising revenue, sponsorships and Patreon.com support).

YouTube is the second most popular website in the world (the first being Google), with over 1 billion users visiting the platform every day. YouTube in its entirety is a global video sharing platform where you are free to upload and share your videos with the rest of the world. Based on the daily user count mentioned above, you can only imagine the amount of content available for browsing, with videos ranging from vlogging (video blogs) to documentaries, movie trailers, news and music; to name a few. With the increasing accessibility of the Internet worldwide and the fact that the Internet plays such an important role in our daily lives, it's no wonder that YouTube offers nearly 1/3 of all users on the Internet globally.

To succeed as a YouTube content creator, you need to identify a few things about yourself and who you want to attract as an audience. Many large YouTube channels have died proverbially in the past due to their changing the theme or content (i.e. topic) of the videos that do not appeal to their already developed and existing fan base. Some aspects to consider when starting a YouTube channel are as follows:

• Decide on a consistent theme that you want to portray in your channel or, if you want to be a news channel that talks about all the latest news, gossip in and around the world or in your area, focus exclusively on that topic.

• Use cleverly titled video names to attract your audience and accompany them with a unique and relevant thumbnail image related to the topic of the video.

• Be presentable and keep your cool when addressing your audience. If you know the topic and speak clearly, users will be more likely to return to your channel to hear what you have to say next.

• Make your channel and content themed around your personality and who you are as an individual. People can spot someone faking it and causing users to withdraw from that content creator.

YouTube can be a great source of income. The platform isn't just there to provide a source of content for users, it's also there to help people make money through it. The entire ecosystem is symbiotic and everyone relies on everyone else; this is what makes YouTube such a strong platform to be associated with. The content creators are what drive the entire community, and it's the content creators that make both YouTube and themselves money.

The four main ways to make money on YouTube are ad support, fan funding, sponsorships/endorsements, and affiliations.

Make sure your videos receive advertising by enabling ad support. This means that you will start earning per video view. Ad support is an integrated software package within YouTube that automatically renders advertisements to provide income to the content creator, based on the number of people watching their videos. Most YouTube content creators use ad support to fund their channel, which in turn allows them to create better quality content, which in turn attracts more users to their channel.

Fan funding is another method of generating an extra revenue stream where your audience can show their support by donating money each month. You can create a fan funding page using patreon.com as a guide, where you are labeled as a creator and supporters as backers.

You can offer them exclusive access to early content, or other supporter rewards that the more they donate, the more they can receive. The size of your rewards for the donation amount is infinite, and this is a great way to earn a little extra on one side.

Another effective method is product sponsorship.

Channelpages.com, Famebit.com, Grapevinelogic.com and other similar websites are the best websites to start with. Product sponsorship or endorsement is where you are offered to promote a product by wearing or having the product displayed in the background of your video. Product endorsement is where you spend a certain amount of time in your video talking about the product and receive payments accordingly from the product supplier.

Number 22: APP CREATION

An application, or an app for short, is a computer program designed to run on mobile devices and computers.

Native mobile apps started life as fun add-ons, especially in the gaming industry. However, the shift in attitude towards apps has been monumental, with some of the biggest companies we know today. When you consider that 89% of consumers' media time is spent on apps, it's easy to see why they have such commercial significance.

Creating your own app is not easy, so you should have some programming experience or hire an app developer. If an app is free, that doesn't mean they don't get any income from it. In-app purchase is one way to earn from a free app.

If someone has installed the app and wants to purchase additional features, they will pay for it. In-app advertising is where you allow your co-creator to advertise on your app. However, there is a method called CPI (cost per install) that makes your app not free. Interested people will buy it and you will get paid for the installation.

Apps are an incredibly good source of income, especially if you already have a great idea for an app that hits one of the 3 E's (educational, fun, efficient). Plus, there's a greater chance that your hard work will pay off as millions of people are always looking for a new and better app to install on their device.

Number 23: PODCAST

Podcasting is a great way for people to connect with their audience. Many YouTube creators have a second channel dedicated exclusively to podcasts.

Podcasts are essentially recordings of yourself discussing something or discussions between two or more people that are then made available for download online for the public to listen to. Think of podcasts as mini talk shows, which can have guests and weekly keynote speakers broadcast different topics that their audience finds interesting.

A podcast can be an audio recording or in video format or both. One user may want to watch the video version of your podcast and have time to sit back and watch the show, or another user may want to download just the audio version of the podcast and listen to it while heading out for their morning run. If you can produce good quality audio recordings of your content, there are plenty of opportunities to be found and noticed on platforms like iTunes with 800 million accounts or SoundCloud which has 250 million users.

If you choose to monetize your podcasts, you have several avenues to go down. Once you've decided which Podcast platform you want to upload to, you'll be given the option of making your podcast available for free or paid download. Most of the top podcasts provide their material for free to maximize their audience reach

Another option is to advertise a digital or physical product or service, either your own or that of a third party. In this case, should a user choose to purchase or download the product that third party advertises through your podcast, you could earn a significant referral fee for recommending someone else's product/service.

Number #24: CREATING MINI COURSES TO SOLVE PROBLEMS

Build a mini-course to help people solve problems or simplify their lives.

As mentioned earlier, online communication and the Internet has become an integral part of our daily lives. We now live in what is referred to as the "digital" or "information" age, which highlights our transition from an industrial to a knowledge-based society. Predictably, with this advancement in the ease of information, online learning has become a very popular way to learn. Students around the world now have access to virtually any course on any topic; that's the best part, it's just the beginning.

If there was ever a "right time" to create your online mini-course, it would be now. Now more than ever, people are hungry for an alternative to the traditional exclusivity of the education system. Mini-courses are highly favored because of their convenience, flexibility, and short time frames.

You don't have to be a professional to create an online mini course. However, you do need to know enough about a topic that you can be fluent, fluid and confident in the way you present the topic, which will make it easier for others to buy your product. Most mini-courses are video-based and include short videos that help people solve specific problems. An example would be "How to Train Your German Shepherd."

As mentioned earlier, you don't need to be an expert. Simply think about the problem your target audience might have and provide them with your knowledge and expertise to overcome that problem. Think about the kinds of common questions people would ask related to your topic of interest.

That said, not all mini-courses have to be about solving a problem. Curiosity is another big factor in attracting people to buy your mini-course. You can adapt existing subjects to make them more entertaining, allowing your audience to approach a particular topic with a completely different approach. An example of this would be to refine an existing hobby technique by giving it your own personal flare to make it more fun or easier to do, a method that worked for you and that you're sure would make the mini-course easier and more engaging for others as well.

Number 25: PHOTOGRAPHS, VIDEO AND MUSIC STOCK

Stock photography, videography and audio jingles to sell on istockphoto, shutterstock, fotolia or similar.

Stock photography is the provision of photos that are often licensed for a specific use. This is useful for people who don't have the budget or time to hire a photographer for creative assignments, instead they can browse a collection of photos for their creative or commercial applications.

Videography applies the same concept, simply in the format of videos. Videographers are often seen on weddings and sporting events. Businesses may need to purchase footage to create corporate events, presentations, promotional videos or advertisements for their company.

Audio jingles are typically short clips that can be purchased for commercial use and advertising. Again, unlike paying royalties to a music artist to use their song, audio jingles are often sold for an average of $19 (about €19), with custom soundtracks ranging between $2,500 and $5,000.

Whatever your field, there are many online sites to sell your work. You have stock sites like istockphoto.com and shutterstock.com that make it easy for hobbyists and amateurs with a passion for photography to start selling their photos online. Once approved as a contributor, most sites don't charge photographers for uploading photos to their portfolios; they take a percentage of each sale.

Most platforms sell multiple types of content such as those listed above, however there are also sites targeted for photos, videos or audio. For example, audio jingles may be sold at audiojingles.net and videos at videohive.net. You may want to try different sites to test your work to increase sales. However, you should keep in mind that companies are willing to take a lower percentage of each sale if you choose to upload exclusively to your own website. So, do your research and find out which approach is best for you.

Chapter 4

ONLINE BUSINESS (ENTERPRISE) -
Starting or buying a business online

Risk factor: **MEDIUM-HIGH**

Reward Factor: **LOW-HIGH**

The following 7 ways to make money online in this section are for people who are entrepreneurial; those who don't mind taking risks and are ready to build something exceptional from scratch or buy an existing business if they have the money to do so. Of course, there are many other types of online businesses you can pursue, but these are some of the most popular online.

Starting an online business can be extraordinarily rewarding. Not only can you get a great sense of pride when you build something from scratch that is successful and creates employment, but you can also build a valuable asset to sell in the future.

Starting an online business can also be very risky. While many people like to think they can do it, the reality is that most people cannot. Most business startups not only fail due to running out of money but can also cause a lot of pressure and stress on the owner(s), sometimes even leading to personal failure.

The secret to success with starting an online business is market and competitive research, realistic budget projections and professional online marketing advice. Don't make assumptions about sales, gross profit margins or operating overhead - research them carefully and make informed projections and judgments.

Number 26: DROPSHIPPING ECOMMERCE BUSINESS

Low risk but good returns possible.

Dropshipping is a retail fulfillment method in which the e-commerce website owner (the merchant) does not hold stock or products themselves and instead relies on a third-party dropshipping warehouse (the supplier) to fulfill orders. The warehouse supplier holds the stock and ships the product directly to the website owners' customers. The supplier dropship warehouse remains completely invisible to the end customer in this entire process.

Anyone can start an online dropshipping business with minimal financial outlay. First of all you should find suppliers who can dropship the products you want to sell. Then you create an e-commerce website on which you place the products (we recommend Shopify for this). Whenever you get a sale and receive payment from the customer, you pass the order details to the supplier and pay them and they then collect, pack and deliver the order to the customer for you.

Fewer capital expenditures and less risk are 2 benefits of running a dropshipping e-commerce business rather than a traditional in-stock e-commerce business. You will still experience complications such as vendor errors, inventory numbers, shipping numbers, and most likely questions about what products will actually be sold.

Number 27: CREATING A SOFTWARE OR APP DEVELOPMENT BUSINESS

In today's high-tech environment, there is no shortage of demand for software development companies to create an app for a business or idea. Approximately 60% of all online traffic now comes from mobile devices, with 89% of the mobile Web being used via apps. So, it's fair to say it's a pretty big (and growing) industry.

Since using apps has become an integral part of our daily communication, information and entertainment, now more than ever people are looking to monetize their next new app idea. Of course, many of those who have an idea for an app, may not have the skills necessary to code said software or app.

You don't need to be an expert designer or app developer to start your own app development business. You simply need an entrepreneurial brain and an aptitude for managing others. This is because you can hire a team of web developers and designers or outsource the work to a freelancer/online team. Your job is to build the business, get customers and market your company, relying on others to produce the goods.

If you have experience in this type of work, people will pay you to create an app or software that they can use as a source of income.

Number 27: CREATING A JOB SITE

Building your membership site is a great way to earn money online simply because it has huge earning potential.

The biggest benefit of running your own membership site is the recurring payments you receive each month. Unlike selling a one-time product, you get paid again and again. Also, when you sell a unique product, you never have the opportunity to build a relationship with your customer. Instead, a membership site allows you to constantly provide new information on a daily, weekly or monthly basis. This builds loyalty and trust with your customer, making it much easier to promote new services or products in the future.

Unlike physical products, you don't need shipping charges, shares to purchase and so on since almost all membership sites provide information as a service. While membership sites are time-consuming and require a lot of planning and setup, the information is free and the cost of running your website is extremely low compared to conventional business setups.

Many membership sites choose to provide a free trial. This provides a win-win situation for both you and your potential client as many people may be interested in your service but are not yet willing to pay. By providing a free trial, you can easily increase your opt-in rate, build trust with doubtful customers, and then have more of those customers convert into paying customers.

As for those who left? There's no additional cost to you. While more members means more money, it's much better to have fewer loyal customers than many customers who drop out after so many months. Think about it, if you have 100 loyal members paying you $30 a month, that's $3,000 a month!

Like most services, you need to think about your target audience for the site, how you will attract them and what will make them stay. Remember, the customer always comes first.

Number #28: CREATING A RESELLER WEB HOSTING BUSINESS

A reseller web hosting is a type of web hosting where the account owner hosts websites through allocated disk space and bandwidth. Resellers are generally web developers or web entrepreneurs and/or web design companies that offer this as part of their extra services. The reseller purchases the host's services on a wholesale basis, then sells them to customers for a profit. The reseller may even have their own product through custom control panels and name servers.

Reseller web hosting companies offer more services and features than a standard service package. Customer account management will be handled by a single account; this simplifies that monthly fees will be charged to customers in reseller plans. The reseller can deploy and rate accordingly, based on the leased space in terms of bandwidth or disk space used.

By having one main admin panel to manage your clients and their personal accounts (i.e. disk space requirements, number of accounts and email domains, etc.), you're keeping overhead costs to a minimum. Each client will have their own admin panel that they can use to manage their personal information such as website, email accounts, etc. as if they were hosted by any other large website host (GoDaddy or Hostgator). While this is a good way to make a very profitable business, there can be shortcomings like in case the host company you are reselling for has problems with its uptime and data servers. You will experience the same problems in this case that will affect your own customers.

Number 29: CREATE A WEB DESIGN BUSINESS

Starting a website design business is not for everyone. Starting any kind of business requires a range of skills, experience and aptitude for the job. You don't have to be an experienced web designer or developer, as you could always employ others, or outsource the work to suitably qualified and experienced people, but you will need to have business acumen. Having business acumen means being able to cope with a wide range of tasks, from sales and marketing to managing employees and teams to finance.

If you're good at selling but don't have Web site design skills, you could perhaps set up a business with one or two people who are good at designing and building Web sites while meeting potential clients and selling your companies services.

The advantages of building a website design business are numerous:
• Almost every business needs a website these days to market themselves and sell online.
• The average website is updated regularly throughout a year, so repeat business is pretty good.
• The average website is usually completely redesigned and rebuilt every 3-5 years.

- Clients usually need help with website marketing, social media and web hosting, so there are other free services you could offer.

You don't have to have an office to start a website design business these days. You could run a remote team to keep costs down with everyone working from home and checking all projects online. Clients usually expect you to visit them rather than them having to visit you.

Chapter 5

ONLINE INVESTMENTS -
Investments and online loans

Risk Factor: **LOW-HIGH**

Reward Factor: **LOW-HIGH**

T he following 5 ways to make money online in this section are for those people who have money to invest or lend to others. So these ways are not time consuming but do require money and some are riskier, but the potential returns can be outstanding.

Online investing can offer incredible returns on investment for very little time and allow you to accumulate considerable wealth over time if everything works in your favor.

Online investing can also be very risky if you don't do your due diligence, don't know or monitor your investments well enough, and if you take too many risks.

The secret to success with online investing is to spread the risks among the investments, perhaps making some higher risk investments that offer the potential for high returns if things go well, but offset these with other lower risk investments that have an almost guaranteed return even if not as favorable.

Number 30: SHARES TRADING

Trading in stocks and shares of large publicly traded companies.

A stock represents a "share" of ownership in a company, which you can buy or sell. When you find a share to buy, you are essentially buying a small stake in a company; in other words, you become a co-owner of the company along with all the other shareholders.

When you are looking to buy stocks, the goal is for the stock to increase in value over time. Essentially, you're trying to buy a share when it's at a low price and then sell it at a later date when the price increases to make a profit. However, this comes with the risk that you will lose your money if the company fails.

What makes stocks so attractive is the fact that this way of deploying money is one of the best long-term investments in the financial market. They tend to outperform many other types of assets including government bonds, corporate bonds and property. In addition, stocks are designed to provide investors with two types of returns, annual income and long-term capital growth.

As we have already established, long-term capital growth simply refers to the value of the unit increasing, providing a profitable return. However, annual income comes in the form of dividends, which are typically paid twice a year. Dividends are a reward for shareholders and are paid when a company is profitable and has cash in the bank.

It should be made clear that stock prices can rise or fall, so buying stocks is never risk-free. Buying stocks is generally (this varies) a long-term investment, so if you want to double your money in one year, buying stocks is probably not the best way to do it. However, if you want to invest for 10 or 20 years, stocks can be a rewarding investment.

Number 31: FOREX TRADING

Foreign exchange, commonly known as "Forex", is the exchange from one currency to another at an agreed upon exchange price in the over the counter market. Forex is the largest market in the world, with an average turnover of over $4 trillion per day.

Essentially, Forex trading is the act of simultaneously buying one currency while selling another. Currency values rise (appreciate) and fall (depreciate) against each other due to various factors including economics and geopolitics. The common goal of forex traders is to profit from these changes in the value of one currency versus another by actively speculating how Forex prices might change in the future.

One of the key elements behind the popularity of Forex is the fact that the Forex market is open 24 hours a day. Unlike most financial markets, the Forex market does not have a physical location or central exchange, but instead encompasses a global network of businesses, banks and individuals.

This means that currency prices constantly fluctuate in value against each other, offering multiple trading opportunities. However, since it is the existence of volatility in the Forex market that allows traders to take advantage of exchange rate fluctuations, traders should be aware that greater volatility also implies greater risk potential.

Forex.com is perhaps the most obvious and recognized Forex trading site with the highest value and reliability.

In summary, Forex trading is not a light and easy money making scheme. It requires time and effort to follow the trading market, learn the system and make smart speculations. However, returns are high or low depending on how much you are willing to risk and invest.

Number 32: CORRELATED BETTING

Matched betting is a betting technique used to profit from free bets and incentives offered by bookmakers. It is generally considered risk-free as it is based on the application of a mathematical equation rather than chance. All bookmakers promote offers (especially during big sporting events) to entice new players to bet with them. They simply place a bet with a bookmaker and then bet against the same outcome in a betting exchange. By covering all possible outcomes, they make guaranteed risk-free profits regardless of the outcome.

There are two parts to matched bets, back bets and lay bets. A back-bet is when we bet on something happening, like betting that Andy Murray will win Wimbledon. If our back-bet wins, we recover our bet plus our winnings. If our back bet loses, we lose our stake. A back bet is when we bet against something happening, such as betting that Andy Murray will not win Wimbledon. If Murray doesn't win Wimbledon, our back bet wins because we bet that he wouldn't win.

The great thing about matched betting is that you can pretty much start with any budget, whether it's €50 or €500. If your starting budget is limited, start with the smaller entry offers and build a stable bankroll. The amount you can earn from matched betting depends on the effort you are willing to put in. The more time you can commit to matched betting, the more money you can make, but even if you can only spare 20 minutes a day, it can easily earn over €400 a month.

Chapter 6

SELL OR RENT WHAT YOU HAVE OR DO

Risk factor: **MEDIUM-LOW**

Reward Factor: **MEDIUM-LOW**

T he following 7 ways to make money online in this section are for those people who just want to make money by selling what they have or do.

Selling or renting what you have or make can be a quick way to earn some extra money and can also lead to other ways to make money online.

Selling or renting what you have or do can also be a bit risky if, for example, your possessions or items are damaged. Make sure you have adequate insurance in place and try to be careful if you're renting something you specifically own.

The secret to making money selling or renting what you have or make is good photography to showcase your property or items and attractive pricing. If you have a premium property or product, of course, you can charge a premium price.

Number 33: SELL WHAT YOU HAVE

Sell what you don't need/want on eBay, Gumtree or similar.

We all own something that we no longer want. Either you bought it, or it was given to you by a friend, family, or acquaintance, and now it's sitting around neglected in your home. Instead of throwing away anything unwanted, why not sell it? It may seem useless to you, but there is bound to be someone out there who is interested.

eBay is one of the most well-known marketplace platforms and people love it because it works so well. As a buyer you can find special deals on things you simply can't find on the high street; eBay opens up the possibilities of what you can find as it's not limited to local garage sales and stores. As a seller, it's a great way to sell unwanted goods, with easy transactions and a ridiculously simple setup for your eBay store (which is a great way to showcase your stuff): all for a small fee for what you sell.

There are endless possibilities for the type of items you could sell on eBay. Do you have clothes that no longer fit but are still in good condition? Maybe you had a collection of comic books or action figures as a child that you no longer use? There are more than 800 million items listed on the eBay marketplace, and with 162 million users - there's bound to be someone who's interested in what you have.

However, ebay.com is not the only option, sites like Gumtree offer a similar but more varied service. Gumtree.com is a marketplace not only for household items but also for vehicles, property, business, pets and services. Unlike eBay, your buyers on Gumtree are likely to be local, so people often prefer to use Gumtree to sell large household items like sofas or pianos, as it would be extremely expensive to try to ship them internationally. Instead, selling such large items on Gumtree allows for local pickup and cash on delivery.

Whichever marketplace you decide to use, both of these sites are easy to use and allow for fast and secure selling and buying of anything.

Number 34: SELL WHAT YOU DO

Sell handmade items on sites you like Etsy or similar.

If you enjoy making crafts and you think others would be interested in buying your handmade items, well, it couldn't be easier. The internet has created a whole host of retail platforms for independent crafters and artisans to promote and sell their products. While some are more popular than others, they all serve the same purpose: to help showcase the skills and creativity of those who perhaps wouldn't get the exposure they deserve elsewhere.

Etsy.com is undoubtedly one of the most popular sites where you can sell handmade items, vintage items and craft supplies. Etsy's creative marketplace has over 24 million buyers with low commissions of just 3.5%. Setting up an Etsy store is simple and easy, requires no monthly fees and has powerful tools that allow you to track your store's statistics such as views, favorites, orders - to improve your store's performance and sales.

However, with the rise of buying handmade crafts online, a number of other sites have sprung up in recent years. Folksy.com is particularly popular in the UK, with over 1.4 million buyers visiting Folksy each month. Unlike Etsy, Folksy works on a monthly subscription service selling only exclusively handmade crafts.

Another alternative is Zibbet.com which, in its own words, aims to help you "purchase unique handmade products, art, vintage and craft supplies." Zibbet's community is smaller, with about 50,000 sellers, however it has features that other independent retail platforms do not. This includes a website builder tool that allows you to create your own professional-looking website to showcase all of your items, as well as a store page on Zibbet's marketplace. In addition, both the website and the marketplace store are seamlessly integrated, making it easy to manage and track inventory and orders from a single administration panel.

Whichever site you decide to choose, this is a brilliant opportunity to turn a beloved hobby into a profitable business. You can improve your skills doing something you love, while being able to share your wonderful creations with people all over the world! I'd say, not bad.

USEFUL LINKS

DIGITAL WORKING

Fiverr.com - Show off your freelance skills

Freelancer.com - Respond to job offers on the platform

Peopleperhour.com - Jobs for freelancers

Guru.com - Jobs for freelancers

Upwork.com - Jobs for freelancers

Microworkers.com - Do small tasks and earn money

Onlinejobs.ph - Virtual assistant

Virtualemployee.com - Virtual assistant

Swagbucks.com - Earn money with surveys

i-say.com - Earn money with surveys

Cashcrate.com - Earn money with surveys

Kgb.com - Answer questions with advice

Justanswer.com - Answer questions with advice

Webanswers.com - Answer questions with tips

Usertesting.com - Earn money by testing websites

Trymyui.com - Earn money by testing websites

Microworkers.com - Complete small jobs

RESIDUAL INCOME (SEMI-PASSIVE)

eToro.com - Benefit from Copy Trading and get automatic income

Clickbank - Earn with Affiliate Marketing

Udemy.com - Make and earn with video courses

Teachable.com - Make and earn with video courses

Istockphoto - Earn with photos

Shutterstock - Earn money with photos

Fotolia - Earn money with photos

ONLINE BUSINESS -
Starting or buying a business online

Wix.com - Create your own website from scratch in 5 minutes

Shopify.com - Make dropshipping with the best online platform

SELL OR RENT WHAT YOU HAVE OR DO

Etsy - Sell your handmade items

Investing Online After the Pandemic

Proven methods to Achieve Super Performance in 2021

BOOK 2

TABLE OF CONTENTS

INTRODUCTION

I f it is true that nowadays it is possible to earn money online, it is also true that often, to take advantage of many methods of earning money, you must necessarily acquire a good knowledge. This can be seen in the world of trading, network marketing, affiliate marketing and many other online businesses.

This of course requires a lot of time to invest in education and often a need to work with mentors, who, in addition to the investment of time, also require a more or less significant investment of money.

But if you purchased this ebook, and are reading it now the reason is simple.

You want to get some extra income or even a second salary without having to spend hours and hours learning techniques and gaining experience but most importantly without having to invest huge capital.

Well, in this book you will find the information you are looking for and it will radically change your life for the better. So let me outline the 3 methods of earning money online:

3 online earning methods that anyone can use, two of which do not require even a DOLLAR of initial investment and that, with a little effort, will give you great personal and especially economic satisfaction. The last method, however, requires an initial investment of about 200 DOLLARS (which, if you do not have immediately, you can get from the other two methods), but that you GUARANTEE 100% a gain ranging from 300 to 500 DOLLARS per month devoting only about twenty minutes a day, maybe after dinner, sitting on the couch with your computer and a good cup of tea.

The purpose of this book, is to get you earning extra income without too many worries other than putting in the effort to understand and apply the methods.

Now, since I'm a pretty practical guy, I'm going to get right to the point with showing you the 3 methods to earn money, without writing pages and pages about the importance of commitment, dedication and perseverance and the fact that nobody gives you anything. Money doesn't fall from the sky all of a sudden.

So read the following chapters carefully, and start applying the tips right away.

Without finding excuses to postpone or procrastinate, you will begin to see, immediately, the first results by dramatically increasing your income.

Well, let's go to the first earning method!

CHAPTER 1

FIRST METHOD OF EARNING ONLINE

www.letsell.com

This is the link to the site that will allow you to adopt the first method of earnings.

This is a method that has given me and continues to give me great satisfaction, a method that does not require, as mentioned above, even a penny of investment. The only thing you have to do is to make your site known, for example through social networks. (don't worry, I'll explain everything from A to Z, and it's very simple and within the reach of anyone)

HOW IT WORKS:

Letsell is a site that allows you to set up , in minutes and for free, a complete e-commerce of thousands of branded products at prices discounted up to 60%, making you immediately earn from sales.

The catalog includes many categories of different products. At your disposal branded clothing, shoes, accessories and cosmetics. Both for men and women.

Once you have activated the e-commerce for free, you will have to start promoting it. The customer then visits the site you promoted, chooses and buys the product, Letsell performs the shipment without you having to make any intermediation and at that point you will receive your percentage of income (from 15% to 30%) directly into your bank account and you will always be able to monitor the progress of your sales through the control panel in the private area of e-commerce.

WHAT YOU HAVE TO DO:

they think of everything: the assortment of products, the organization of the warehouse and orders, shipments and returns. Everything is managed by the Letsell team, which includes professionals with great experience in the field of e-commerce. You just have to take care of promoting your business and in the next pages I will explain how to do it. The requirements to start an e-commerce on Letsell's platform are: to be 16 years of age or older, to have completed your schooling, and to be an American resident.

ACCOUNT TYPES:

On Letsell you can choose from 3 account options:

- FREE - the FREE account allows you to start selling right away, for free, in minutes. It is free forever and allows you to earn an average of up to 15% on sales and receive up to 10 orders per month.

- BASIC - BASIC account costs $8.25 per month per annual subscription. It allows you to earn on average up to 30% on sales and receive up to 100 orders per month. Other benefits come from the ability to customize more of the e-commerce and being able to have more products on display.

- PRO - the PRO account is priced at €16.60 per month for an annual subscription. It allows you to earn on average up to 30% on sales and receive unlimited orders. You have the maximum performance and functionality available, allows you to sell in addition to fashion products, even children's toys and creams. It also allows greater customization of your e-commerce site.

Obviously, at the beginning, the best account is definitely the FREE one, I myself started with it because of the convenience and the total absence of expenses, and then switch to the BASIC one, once I made the first sales and received the first earnings, and with which I still operate comfortably.

STEP BY STEP PROCEDURE:

I'm now going to walk you through, step-by-step, what you need to do to open your e-commerce on Letsell.

Once you arrive at www.letsell.com, click on start now. Enter an email, password and the name you want to give to the store.

Once registered, your site is already online! Easy no?

Well, at this point you can access the control panel, from which you must configure your e-commerce site.

In the section site configuration (on the right of the screen), you will have to choose the domain name, the title of the site and insert a logo. To create the logo, just click on "tutorial" and follow the instructions. You can do this in a few minutes and without any difficulty.

Finally click on "save".

In the advanced configuration section, you will have to enter the subtitle and the description of the site, and in the box "google analytics" enter the following tracking ID: UA-000000-1.

Finally click on "save".

In the profile section you will have to insert your personal information and the bank information, that is the account where you will be credited with all your earnings!

You will then simply enter the ACCOUNT NUMBER of a bank account associated with you or a normal prepaid card or debit card with ACCOUNT NUMBER associated such as hype card or N26 (I use N26, debit card very convenient and completely free).

free).

Then click on "save".

Done! Your e-commerce site is completed. A quick and easy operation I would say. Now, let's talk about how to promote it.

PROMOTION:

Promoting your e-commerce site is definitely the most important part of this online earning method. To earn money, you need to make your site known to as many people as possible, and what better way than social networks? Yes, social networks are certainly the main and best tools to make your business through Letsell take off and make you earn a lot of money.

Let's start by saying that I mainly use Instagram and Facebook, in principle what you need to do is create a profile with the name of your site, and then create a page in both social platforms in which you will then constantly publish product photos, flyers and offers.

Instagram and Facebook have different tools for promoting and attaching your business, very useful for creating posts that direct your contacts directly to the products you are talking about, in order to facilitate their purchase.

In the personal area of Letsell, you will find at your disposal photos of the products and promotional photos to publish directly and easily. You can also directly make screens of the products, and share them explaining, in the description of the post, for example, the sizes and colors available, prices and discounts and various details.

Always in the personal area of Letsell you can find very useful and enlightening tutorials on how to manage and use social networks in the best way.

Do not forget of course to insert the link to your site that will bring potential customers directly on the platform.

All you have to do is to make your instagram and facebook pages grow and become known by following the various profiles of more or less famous clothing brands, putting the right hashtags under the posts you publish and constantly publishing posts, stories and content.

Once the target of people interested in your products, will notice them and will start to make the first orders, you will start to earn, and meanwhile you will start to find customers who, over time, will become attached to your e- commerce site and will buy what they need from you. Ensuring you in this way, as well as increasing earnings, even constant earnings over time!

This was the first method of earning, with which you will earn part of your second salary. Now let's move on to the second!

CHAPTER 2

SECOND METHOD OF EARNING ONLINE

www.kdp.amazon.com

This will be the site that leads to the platform that you will use to perform what I will tell you about this second method of earning online.

For the latter, in fact, you will have to go and take advantage of the completely free platform that Amazon makes available to all global writers.

Kindle Direct Publishing, in fact, allows book authors to publish their works both in digital format and in paper form, also providing many useful tools to, for example, create the cover of your ebook.

As mentioned above, also in this second method you won't have to make any initial or future investment.

The only thing you have to invest is a little bit of your time, which, once it bears fruit, will guarantee you a passive income over time and, if you want, an increasing one.

It is therefore to write one or more ebooks (digital books), and then, once completed, just upload them for free on the platform of kdp and that's it. Your ebook will be visible and available to millions of readers across America that will guarantee you a nice monthly income and especially passive.

Obviously this is a more than scalable business since, if you want to earn more money, all you have to do is write more ebooks! And think how much your earnings can increase if, over time, you can write and publish 5, 10 or 20 ebooks!

Remember that once you've written and published, you won't have to do anything but enjoy your earnings, which will come passively while you go about the other daily activities of your day or even while you sleep soundly!

Now you're probably thinking the typical "easy to say" phrase, you're probably thinking that you, most likely, don't know how to write a book and especially that you don't have the slightest idea of what topics to cover. Don't worry, as you read on you'll realize that it's easier than it sounds. Before writing my first ebook, I myself had the same limiting ideas that led me to procrastinate over time until the day I decided to start and in which I realized that it was not so difficult to write an ebook, indeed.

In a few days of work, my first creature was finished and, after all the necessary corrections, I published it immediately obtaining excellent economic satisfaction that still yields me a monthly income that will increase by adding to my inventory other ebooks, including this one.

I remind you that you don't have to write 300-page comedies, but you must, through your knowledge of a particular topic, write an ebook that answers in a simple and concise way to questions that people ask and providing a solution to their problems. You bought this ebook because you intend to get some extra income, and well here you have found and are finding solutions to your problem.

The same thing you need to do.

Remember that a lot of the information people want can often be found for free online, but very few people want to spend hours and hours searching through the thousands of sources on the web today, so they prefer to buy an ebook that is a compilation of all that information in one place, saving them valuable time.

That being said, I'm sure you specialize in a certain field, everyone does. There must surely be a topic for which you, know more about than most people, well the latter is the right one for your first ebook.

COSTS AND EARNINGS:

As mentioned above the author does not have to incur any expenses to publish on KDP. However, the moment sales are made, commissions are charged.

The percentage of earnings, called "royalty", varies depending on the price at which you sell your ebook:

- if you would sell it at a price ranging from $0.99 to $2.99, the percentage of profit would be 35%

- if you sell it at a price that exceeds 2.99 DOLLARS, the profit percentage will be 70%.

STEP BY STEP PROCEDURE:

The first thing you need to do is obviously write your ebook. So choose the topic on which you want to form your work and then make a list of all the various macro topics with which you want to divide it. At this point you make a sort of momentary summary to help you follow an order and finally start to get all the information you need on that topic documenting on the net, on YouTube or through other books.

Remember, everything must be your own, do not copy verbatim what you have learned from your sources but modify it by adding your personal experiences, the advice you find most useful, etc.

The time has come to write, write and write some more. Open a page on word and start. Dedicating a few hours a day, your ebook will be ready in less than a week. Time well spent!

Yes, because once finished, the earnings from your work will be closer and closer.

Once the ebook is finished, a crucial part is the correction. Reread it all making any changes and correcting errors. In this phase you can get help from friends and relatives, having them read your book and taking their advice and criticism as gold, so as to make your creation even better.

At this point you have arrived at the last step:

PUBLICATION:

Before you can publish your ebook on Amazon's platform, you will have to register or log in to it. So connect to the main page of KDP, and click on the Register button, then choose the option Create your KDP account and enter the requested data.

If you already have an account that you use to make purchases on Amazon, you can use the same credentials to access KDP by clicking on Login and entering your email and password.

Once in the main screen, click on Update in the box The account information is not complete. Enter all the required information including personal, fiscal and related to the Reception of payments that is the code ACCOUNT NUMBER, BIC and the name of the bank. As in the first method, you can use your own bank account or any debit card with an associated ACCOUNT NUMBER.

Well now that your KDP account is complete, you can move on to publishing your ebook. Click on the Library tab, then choose the Ebook kindle option and specify the language, book title and subtitle in the appropriate field.

Enter the author's data in the first and last name fields.

In the Description section, enter an attractive description in which you present your book in the best possible way, since this will be visible on the Amazon product page.

In the next screens you will have to enter 7 keywords that reflect the type of your ebook. Then you will be given the possibility to create a cover in the ebook kindle cover section at the option Use cover creation.

Finally fill in the last steps and click the Publish your Kindle eBook button.

And that's it, within 72 hours, your work will be available on the Kindle Store ready and available for millions of readers. The first Earnings will not be long in coming and with them also a great personal satisfaction for the work done.

This was the second method of earning money online. Through these first two methods you can already secure some great extra income.

But now let's move on to the third method, with which you will have a fixed income ranging from 300 to 500 DOLLARS per month!

CHAPTER 3

THIRD METHOD OF EARNING ONLINE + INITIAL SURPRISE

W e now come to the third method to earn online, my favorite because of its ease and especially its security in receiving from 300 to 500 DOLLARS per month.

Not to mention the 1500 dollars (and here's the surprise) that you can get the first month of activity!

This is Matched Betting, which translated into American means "matched bets".

But don't worry, I assure you that it has nothing, but nothing to do with betting, gambling and other earning methods with which you can lose a lot of money.

Here we are talking about a mathematical method, absolutely Sicilian and 100% legal, by continuing to read you will understand everything.

Matched Batting is a technique that allows you to earn from bonuses offered by betting sites. But it is not a bet at all. How?

Let's take a simplified example:

Suppose you bet, by flipping a coin, 10 DOLLARS on the exit of "heads" and then simultaneously bet another 10 DOLLARS on the exit of "tails". At this point, whether "heads" or "tails" comes up, my profit will be zero. So I will end up with my initial 20 DOLLARS, no more and no less. But this is where Matched Betting comes into play, taking advantage of welcome bonuses.

The betting sites in fact, to encourage new customers to use their platforms, often offer welcome bonuses that can be withdrawn once at least one bet has been placed.

Going back to the initial example of the coin, if I bet 10 dollars of my own on the fact that "heads" comes out and another 10 dollars, this time not mine but of the bonus, on the fact that "tails" comes out, the 20 dollars that I will get will be composed of my initial 10 dollars plus the 10 dollars of the bonus given to me by the site, thus guaranteeing me a gain of 10 dollars.

Now, assuming you understood something about it, (it's much simpler than it sounds) this was the basic concept of Matched Betting, there are other facets, starting with the fact that you don't bet by throwing coins, but mainly on soccer.

You may be thinking that this is not a feasible thing to do since you've probably never made any bets and maybe don't even remotely follow soccer. Well, when I discovered this method of earning money I was in the same precise condition described, but I assure you that to earn with Matched Betting, knowing how to bet and knowledge of soccer are of little use. This is because you are guided step by step by online consulting sites that will allow you to earn easily by providing you with the right tools and telling you exactly what to do and when to do it.

One of the consulting sites in question, the one I use myself, is called Bluesheep (www.bluesheep.it). And it is Bluesheep that will provide you with the necessary tools and guides to do Matched Betting, after you have activated the monthly subscription of 15 DOLLARS (at the moment). But don't worry, you won't have to pay a penny because the site, Bluesheep, allows you to take advantage of their service for two welcome offers that will earn you about 20 DOLLARS so you can verify that Matched Betting really works, understand how it works and if you are satisfied you can subscribe without spending anything out of your pocket!

In addition, for any problem or question you can contact them via message and in a few minutes they will respond and help you.

I invite you to take a look at the site, where you will better understand everything.

COSTS, INITIAL INVESTMENT AND EARNINGS:

The only cost to apply the technique of Matched Betting is the monthly subscription to the consulting site, which, as mentioned above, you can avoid by using the earnings from the free trial. In the future you will support this small monthly expense with the fixed and continuous earnings you will get.

The initial investment to take advantage of the free trial is about 30 DOLLARS, while once subscribed, the expenditure sufficient to start is about 200 DOLLARS (money that, if you do not have, you can get from the two methods of earning online described in previous chapters).

As for the earnings from using this third method, these will be fixed, insured and recurring over time.

As mentioned above, if you are not already registered to any betting site, you will earn in just the first 1 or 2 months

up to 1500 dollars thanks to the rich welcome bonus. If you are already registered on several sites, no problem, there are many recurring bonuses that will allow you to earn from 300 to 500 dollars per month.

TIME TO SPEND PER DAY:

Once you get the hang of it, I assure you that the time to devote to this activity is around 20 minutes per day (it is important to devote some time every day to make the most of this opportunity and thus to earn the most).

RISK? INESISTENT:

In Matched Betting the risk is zero. All the actions that you are going to take, following the instructions of Bluesheep guides, are based on mathematical calculations (which you do not have to do yourself. Everything will be done through the tools provided) that allow you to cancel the risk and ensure a constant and recurring gain.

Let's be clear, as soon as I heard about this method about a year ago, I too was skeptical (as you most likely will be), it's human nature. But after reading up on the web (there are many testimonials that talk about and explain Matched Betting, from popular Youtubers to Facebook groups, to sites like Wikipedia, The Guardian, Huffpost...) and understanding what it was all about, I decided to give it a try and the satisfaction, along with the gains, came immediately.

Being skeptical is not a bad thing, but it is important to get informed and understand everything about a particular topic before giving a final opinion.

In this case trust me. I assure you that Matched Betting works and it is a technique that has been used for a long time in several countries, especially in England, but only in the last 2 or 3 years it has started to spread to America.

So, what are you waiting for! It's time to take action and start earning part of your second salary with Matched Betting!

STEP-BY-STEP PROCESS:

First of all, since everything will be done through the consulting site, go to www.bluesheep.it and make the

free registration.

Then click on the Register button at the top right, enter all the required data and click again on the Register button.

Once you have registered and logged in with your credentials, you will find yourself in a screen showing the various steps to be taken.

You will also have at your disposal 5 free guides each consisting of videos and written explanations, which I highly recommend you to view, as they are quite concise but full of information that will make you understand further everything about the Matched Betting in detail.

Once you've finished the guides, it's time to earn your first $20 or so by using the two promotions in the Welcome Offers section. Follow the directions that you find which will lead you, step by step, to your first earnings.

Once you've done this, after having understood and become familiar with the technique, you just have to subscribe using the money earned from the first two promotions then starting to complete the other welcome offers coming to earn, as previously mentioned, about 1500 dollars in the first weeks of activity and then move on to recurring offers that will ensure you a few hundred dollars every month!

Well for this third method of earning online is all, I hope I was clear, because I think it is a valid and excellent opportunity.

Let's go to the bonus method!

CHAPTER 4

BONUS METHOD, LOOK TO THE FUTURE

And here we are talking about the last method of earning online, the bonus method.

Bonus because it is a method that does not give you an immediate profit, but in the future, it could give you instead a great or very great gain.

It's all very simple, all you have to do is download an application to your smartphone or tablet, make a simple registration and click on a button. Then you only have to keep the application open throughout the day to earn real money in the form of Electroneum (I'll explain below what they are).

The application won't affect your device's battery life or internet consumption via your data connection.

By naming Electroneums (whose abbreviation ETN), you are talking about cryptocurrencies.

ETN is precisely a cryptocurrency or cryptocurrency, founded by Richard Ells in November 2017.

A cryptocurrency is an equal, decentralized, digital currency whose implementation relies on the principles of cryptography to validate transactions and the generation of currency itself.

Decentralized control of each cryptocurrency works through a generalized ledger technology called blockchain, which serves as a database of public financial transactions.

One of the many cryptocurrencies you're sure to be familiar with or have heard of is Bitcoin.

Now, in order for an individual to earn, a portion of a cryptocurrency, he or she must perform an operation called mining (in jargon, it is therefore said that he or she must mine a cryptocurrency.).

Mining (or creation) is the way cryptocurrencies use to issue currency.

The Bitcoin network, for example, but also the networks of other cryptocurrencies, stores transactions within data structures called "blocks" in jargon. In order for a block to be added to the blockchain, i.e. the public database that contains all the transactions of that particular cryptocurrency, it is necessary for a miner (or processor) to "close" it by finding a certain code that is in turn located through many attempts and mathematical algorithms. This process "crystallizes" the block preventing any future modification. Whoever finds this code, i.e. the miner, is rewarded with a certain amount of cryptocurrency.

The operation of mining a cryptocurrency today is very complex. In fact, it involves a huge consumption of electricity and processes that are very difficult to carry out by DIY.

That's why I'm going to explain how to take advantage of Electroneum technology.

As mentioned above Electroneum is a new cryptocurrency founded recently, which differs from the others because of the ease with which it can be mined, thus making a real gain.

To mine this cryptocurrency is in fact sufficient to install the application that I mentioned at the beginning, keep it open as much as possible making sure that automatically through the servers and the CPU of the smartphone, perform the operation of minig and then accumulate an increasing amount of currency, which you're going to turn into real profits in dollars through simple steps that I will expose shortly.

Below is the image with the appearance of the application that is called precisely Electroneum and that you can find and install directly from the appstore of your mobile device.

STEP BY STEP PROCEDURE:

Well, after installing the application and performing the simple registration, you will find yourself in its main screen, in which will be visible, at the bottom, four different menus:

1. Miner - this is the menu where you can activate and start mining cryptocurrency. Doing so is very simple, just click on the button "start cloud mining" located in plain sight at the bottom even if it is often already active automatically. You can check the latter possibility by viewing, in the same screen, the indication "cloud mining ACTIVE" or "cloud mining OFFLINE".

   Once activated the mining, you will be already earning Electroneum and you just have to leave the app open in the background.

   On average you'll be earning 2 to 5 Electroneum per day. This depends from one mobile device to another. The Electroneums earned at this stage are considered "outstanding balance". They will then be transferred to your wallet and then given directly to you once you reach the minimum payment amount of 100 ETNs.

2. Wallets - once you reach 100 ETNs in your outstanding balance, your mined Electrneum will be transferred to your wallet. In this section you will find all your Electroneum earned by mining and you can start the process of converting them into real money, in DOLLARS! (I will explain the steps soon).

3. Value - in this menu you will find, always updated in real time, the value of an Electroneum compared to physical currencies such as dollars, dollars, etc. ...

and it is here that the real meaning of this bonus method comes into play, i.e. looking to the future.

Let me explain: at the time I'm writing this ebook, an Electroneum is worth about 0.006 DOLLARS (1 ETN = 0.006 EUR).

Now, approximately in a month of mining you should be able to earn about 100 ETN that multiplied by 0.006 are worth 0.60 cents (100 ETN x 0.006 = 0.60 USD), a ridiculous amount.

But the cryptocurrency market, is constantly fluctuating minute by minute, with increases and decreases of up to 1000% in a day! That said, therefore, it is more than realistic the possibility that tomorrow 1 Electroneum could be worth 1 DOLLARS, thus going from a value of 0.60 cents to 100 DOLLARS. In one month, 1 Electroneum could be worth 100 Dollars, going from 100 Dollars of profit to 10.000 Dollars! And so on.

In 2009 a single unit of Bitcoin cryptocurrency was worth less than 0.001 cents of

DOLLARS. Today 1 single Bitcoin is worth more than 3,470 DOLLARS and this explains how all the people who bought even small amounts back in the day are now millionaires!

In this method of earning bonuses I have shown you a system with absurd potential without having to spend now or in the future even a penny! Considering also that the Elecroneum is a young currency with intriguing prospects and very good.

4. Other - in this menu you will find various information related to your profile.

HOW TO CONVERT ETN INTO DOLLARS:

The key part, the one that I think you're most interested in, is how to transform the mined Electroneum in your wallet into real money to be withdrawn directly from your credit/debit card.

Well, let's see the steps to take:

1. Register for free at www.kucoin.com - kucoin is a cryptocurrency exchange platform.
2. Locate on Kucoin, among the various crypto coins, the Electroneum, click on it to find in this way your unique alphanumeric address to be entered then in the application of Electroneum in the, Wallet menu by clicking in the section "pay".

After confirming, you will have, free of charge, moved your ETNs from the Electroneum application to the Kucoin platform.

Once you move your Electroneum to Kucoin, through this platform, they will be converted into Bitcoin which is the cryptocurrency par excellence.

3. Finally you have to open a free account on the site www.coinbase.com - Coinbase is the most famous cryptocurrency wallet in the world, on which, after connecting to the account a credit/debit card, you can transform the share of Bitcoin in real currency that is in DOLLARS.

4. To do this you will have to enter the Bitcoin code of Kucoin on Coinbase.

The procedure may seem a bit 'complex but I assure you that with a little practice will become simple and fast. The interfaces of the two platforms (Kucoin and Coinbase) are intuitive and user-friendly.

That said, run and download the Electroneum app and start mining. Know that if you want you can also buy a sum directly on Kucoin (with 10 DOLLARS you buy more than 1,500), the choice is yours. As for me I have already accumulated more than 300 only with the application and without having spent a penny.

Earnings vary and can reach high daily figures, so I suggest you to periodically check the value of ETNs compared to the DOLLAR to take advantage of any rises. And who knows how much our Electroneum will be worth in a month, 6 months or a year! We will see!

CHAPTER 5

FINAL CONSIDERATIONS

A nd here we are at the last chapter of this ebook, so let me express some final thoughts:

Summing it all up in a few words, I've revealed to you 3 working methods, tried and tested by myself. Methods that I still use and that, at the end of each month, allow me to put a large sum of money in my pocket, a real salary by devoting no more than an hour a day.

Reaching 1000 DOLLARS per month with these methods is not at all difficult, and exceeding them is very possible, provided, of course, that you commit yourself to understand them and then put them into practice in the best possible way.

It's useless to tell you that money doesn't fall from the sky and that nobody gives you anything, I think you know that. It takes commitment, perseverance and determination to earn and change your life, as for any other area outside the economic one.

Well, I have provided you with the right tools, now it's your turn. Finish these few lines and then start your life change from an economic and financial point of view.

I wish you great gains and great personal satisfaction.

AMAZON DEEPENING

AMAZON ARBITRAGE

Arbitrage is a behavior that allows you to profit from situations of inconsistency in the pricing system or regulatory or fiscal differentiations between institutional or territorial entities.

The simplest inconsistency is linked to the existence of different prices for a single good on different markets. The arbitrageur, i.e., the person making the arbitrage, buys the asset on the market where the price is lower and resells it on the one where it is higher, profiting from the difference.

Logically this situation cannot last long, because it is the activity of the arbitrageur to increase the demand where the cost is lower and the offer is higher, thus generating a rebalancing of prices.

Therefore, the main reason for the existence of arbitrage consists in an inefficiency of the markets, finding what costs less in one market and reselling it with an increase in price in another.

The advantage of this practice is enormously amplified by the online factor; e-commerce in itself is a much larger market than the store around the house or the big distribution.

It is possible to sell a product online covering not only the United States, but it is also possible to extend the possibility of selling in the main countries of the world.

The third advantage is to make available a particular item that the traditional store cannot offer. It is easier for a customer to buy on the internet, not because he finds a price advantage, but because he finds the product he is interested in and cannot find otherwise close to home.

The combination of market breadth and product that is not possible to find close to home makes it possible to sell items defined as niche, i.e. those products characterized by a very narrow audience that does not meet the profit margins of traditional trade, but that can be profitable if proposed on a larger scale.

Among the marketplaces (Amazon, eBay, etc..) the price differences are many and often the consumer does not have time to compare different listings or prefer to rely on the guarantee offered by a specific channel (for example, if I have activated Amazon Prime I will prefer to buy from that channel).

E-commerce arbitrage guarantees limited margins to the seller who cannot make mistakes: continuing to publish an ad without realizing that the source has changed the price or put the item out of stock, inserting products with a good margin but with little appeal among consumers, etc.

FINDING PRODUCTS - The best items for sale in Arbitrage are books, mainly because they guarantee acceptable margins and are not products that are returned and run into technical problems, as could happen to Bluetooth headphones, for example. Also, books are not "seasonal" and do not chase particular fashions; in short, they always sell.

The books that are most popular on Amazon are those with manual content, i.e. for learning a specific subject. In order not to run into fierce competition, I recommend that you focus on out-of-print books, which can be sold at a higher price than the cover price, despite being used.

Scout out used book markets with the help of the Amazon App, so you can scan the barcode and immediately check the sale price. Verisimilarly the cost of the book should be at most 1/7th of the price you would like to set, also having to pay delivery and the Amazon commission of 15%.

THE WORLD OF REVIEWS

The world of reviews is an all under-the-table business that you can leverage for revenue that really can't be underestimated.

For sellers to get reviews on Amazon is not at all easy, it is estimated that out of 100 orders only 6% of customers leave a review, for this reason to launch a product on the market you need to find reviews that serve to have a social proof, albeit fake, through gray methods.

They are called gray methods precisely because they are right against Amazon's Terms of Service.

Sure it's unethical to give 5 star reviews for a product that doesn't deserve them, but consider that Amazon customers, once they've found the product to be poor quality and inadequate, can request a return and receive their money back without waiting for the seller's approval.

Amazon sellers to find these 5-star reviews take advantage of the communities of Facebook groups and Telegram channels dedicated entirely to Amazon reviews. Just search on Facebook for "Amazon Review" to get a quick look at how many there are. Ask to join and after a few days you'll be accepted, provided you've answered the questions of the administrators.

A tip to get you accepted faster: don't use newly created accounts with fancy names, you'll be seen as no good. Once you're in, you'll notice the amount of products available for review that you can receive at your home at no cost.

Camcorders, watches, Bluetooth headphones, irons, belts, anything and everything that Amazon sellers can offer you for free in exchange for a 5 star review with a few photos. A minimum knowledge of English is required to communicate with sellers, who 80% of the time are Chinese selling on Amazon.it.

Here's how it works: you find a product available for review, contact the seller saying you are interested and attach a screenshot of your Amazon profile and he will tell you if you are eligible or not.

Then he will send you the keyword to find the product and you will have to buy it, paying in advance with your payment card simulating a real purchase. Once the order is placed, you must send the order number to the seller.

After a few days you will receive the item at home, and to write the review you must wait at least 3-4 days after delivery so as not to make Amazon's algorithm suspicious.

Since a few months now, the system slows down the publication of reviews by a couple of days, so don't worry that this one doesn't go online right away. When it does, you'll get an email notification and you'll need to send the link to your review to the seller. Within 2-3 days, he will send you a full refund via Paypal.

Right now you're breaking even, so your expenses are equal to your revenue, however, you have a product in your home that most likely won't do you any good and has enough sales value to make a profit.

For this reason, in order to generate earnings, you can put it up for sale on Ebay or Amazon using the existing title and photos.

Obviously, I recommend lowering the sale price by a few dollars to create convenience and make money quickly.

Once the sale has been made, I recommend the service of Spediamo.it, a very cheap site that allows you to send parcels with home pickup and delivery in 24h-48h through the express courier SDA. The lowest rate is 6.78 dollars.

Well, now imagine that you activate not just for one product, but for many items in the same week, possibly expensive, from $50 upwards, which then guarantee high profits by removing the shipping.

It is essential not to request the return to Amazon to get another refund, which apart from being a scam against the seller, will lead you to be reported in the black-list of reviewers and in the long run leads to the ban also from Amazon, which preserves itself from dishonest buyers who send back almost all of the products they buy.

Unfortunately, Amazon tries to block not only those who make many returns, but all customers who write reviews that are biased, which is why you need to follow a number of steps to keep yourself from getting caught.

1. Never buy the product from the links the seller sends you, precisely because Amazon can recognize that all the traffic coming from Facebook leads to 5 star reviews, and can find you out quickly. Search for the product normally on Amazon and you'll be on the safe side.

2. Don't write more than one review a day.

3. Don't write too short reviews, but don't write too long reviews either, and try to focus on something a potential buyer wants to know about the item (you don't have to praise the item too much even though you are required to put 5 stars as a rating). This way you'll get "helpful votes" that will allow you to have a healthier Amazon profile and you can also move up in the special reviewer ranking, which depends precisely on the number of helpful votes you receive.

How do I get eligible to do reviews?

The minimum requirements to be so are not impossible to meet, first of all you need to have purchased on Amazon products for at least 50 Dollars and have written on your profile at least 5-6 reviews for products purchased for yourself, so outside of the talk of Facebook groups.

Set up in your Amazon profile a photo, a short bio about who you are and obviously your first and last name.

A non-essential requirement is to be a Prime subscriber, but consider that sellers do not reimburse you for shipping costs, so it is worth subscribing, even to receive packages very quickly. Prime's free trial period is 30 days, after which it costs $36 per year, or $5 per month.

Why aren't Chinese sellers responding to me?

Chinese sellers are almost all located in Shenzhen, a metropolis that is 7 hours ahead of Rome's time zone. That's why, in order to chat with Chinese people, it's better to connect in the morning, from 7 am until noon at the latest, to find them online. Otherwise you'll have to wait until the next day and the time will be much longer.

HOW TO SELL ON EBAY - If you have no experience in selling, starting to sell on Ebay is not difficult. After you sign up, click on "Sell" to create a listing.

Enter the title, select the product condition as "new," upload the photos you downloaded from Amazon, and if it asks for the EAN put "NOT APPLICABLE."

Also copy the description from Amazon and enter the various features, and then list the sale price in a "buy it now" format and I recommend allowing buyers to send a proposal to sell faster.

Select 30 days for the duration of the listing and as a method of payment Paypal, although you have to pay 3.4% commission on the money you receive. As for the courier, select "Other 48h Courier" and the packing time you prefer, but I suggest you hold on tight and offer free shipping.

The cost for posting the listing is $0.37, payable every 30 days, while Ebay will charge you 10% of the cost of the product at the time of sale, which is deducted each month from the payment method on which you receive the money from sales revenue.

ALTERNATIVE METHODS TO FIND PRODUCTS TO RESELL

There are 3 sites to get Amazon products discounted almost 100% and then you can resell them wherever you want. I'm talking about Testzon, EliteDealClub and Vipon.

TESTZONE - TestZone is a site with hundreds of items available on Amazon, for which you can get a coupon even without having to leave a review. At first, you won't be able to get the most expensive items, as you need a lot of "EXP" points, or experience, for those. You'll have to make your bones with less expensive products to accumulate EXP points, but that's not always the case anyway, it depends from seller to seller.

Once you've found a product you're interested in, click on "More Info", then on "Test Product". In the chat box that appears, write that you are interested in taking the item and that you are available to leave a review on Amazon.

After a while you will receive confirmation and the coupon to purchase the item.

ELITE DEAL CLUB - EliteDealClub is my favorite site to find the best Amazon deals, without the requirement to write reviews.

New deals come out every day and you'll have to be super quick to snag them. Once you sign up, every morning at 9:30am you'll get a newsletter listing all the products available starting at 10am, with the purchase price very often being $1 if not $0.

The most convenient thing about Elite Deal Club is that the code is forwarded to you as soon as you request it, although very often the deals run out in no time.

VIPON - Vipon is the site with the most deals on Amazon, but they're mostly for items that are shipped by the seller, so they don't ship with Prime. The deals are generally less advantageous than those presented within the two previously mentioned sites, but you can explore the offers in the other marketplaces as well, and order items from other countries and enter your shipping address.

HOW TO PUT PRODUCTS UP FOR SALE

To start selling on Amazon, first you'll need to open a seller account. There are two sales plans:

-Basic: recommended if you make less than 40 sales per month, on which you'll pay 1 Dollar fixed cost and commission on the sale price that can reach up to 15% for some categories. With the basic sales plan you will still be able to join Amazon's logistics, but you won't be able to ship a new product in their catalog to their warehouse, like a private label product.

-Pro: This is the account of those who are serious about their business. The subscription costs $39 per month and has no additional fixed costs, but the commission remains as a percentage of the product cost. You'll have access to a plethora of services on the seller's platform that you can't use with the basic plan, like the whole promotions section.

You'll be able to switch from one plan to another at any time, but I suggest you start with the basic account to navigate more calmly and make the SellerCentral functions more familiar to you.

You will also need to indicate a credit card in the name of the same person/company, but it is proven that the system also accepts some debit cards, as long as they are cards/account, so even with the iban.

Once inside your SellerCentral click on "Catalog">"Add Products" and add the ASIN of the product you want to sell. The ASIN is the 8-character alphanumeric code found in the Amazon product links, or simply by scrolling down the page you can find it in the "More Info" section. One ASIN is for example B01DVVY81Q.

If there are no category restrictions, you'll be able to create your own offer by adding the price, the condition of the item, and whether you'd prefer to have Amazon handle the shipping or you'd prefer to take care of it yourself, with your trusted courier. In this case, you will have to modify the "Shipping Model", establishing the cost for each delivery service, and the delivery time of the package.

When you receive an order, you'll see it in the "Orders" section, or by downloading the "Amazon Seller" app, you'll be notified on your phone.

As for profits from sales, they will be available net of Amazon commissions 7 days after the last delivery date to the customer, but if you're just starting out you may have to wait up to 21 days to be able to move the money to your bank account. This is a major flaw for those selling on Amazon, but on the other hand it protects consumers for a possible refund.

AMAZON FBA

Amazon FBA is a business that has broken out in the United States in recent times, to which both many simple people without entrepreneurial experience and merchants who have discovered the online late are approaching. FBA is nothing but the logistics of Amazon, in fact it stands for "Fulfillment by Amazon". Simply put, FBA works like this: You sell, Amazon ships.

The service is based on these 5 cornerstones:

1. The seller ships their products to an Amazon logistics center, where they will be stored;

2. Amazon stores how many units are available within the warehouse and offers them for sale on the site; 3.When a customer orders, Amazon packs and ships the sold products through its network of couriers; 4.The system will provide both the seller and the customer with the tracking code of the package;

5.Amazon Staff will handle customer service for the seller, including filing for returns.

If you don't have anything of your own to put in the FBA logistics, the easiest thing to do is to import products from China that already have a market on the internet, or maybe you could come up with something that could be useful and can't be found on Amazon. Think of some product that you were looking for for you but couldn't find, or you were forced to buy it despite having negative reviews, just because you had no choice. Here, this could be an idea of a product to put up for sale.

If you're unimaginative, you can find something interesting to sell within an unsaturated niche, i.e. with little supply, by importing it from Chinese factories. The most popular site to put you in touch with these suppliers is called Alibaba. Once your first product is on sale, it won't be difficult to invoice just with this 3000 Dollars per month. Be careful though, because the margins of a merchant are around 30% (you'll find out later). That's why you'll have to look for new profitable products and launch them on Amazon, in order to multiply your earnings.

This is the coolest part of Amazon FBA: being a scalable business, you can earn more and more money month after month by investing some of the money you earned.

Another upside is the low business risk. Imagine that you want to open a business in your city: rent, electricity, water, furniture, municipal expenses, personnel are all expenses that you will have to face immediately (excluding the goods to be sold), for an expenditure that is around 20 thousand dollars. Amazon, on the other hand, asks you for a "rent" of its back office, that is the platform to put the products on sale, which amounts to $ 39 per month, all inclusive. In addition, with Amazon you will reach not only passers-by and the inhabitants of your city, but the entire population who shop online, and nowadays Amazon is the search engine for online shopping, you do not even use Google anymore.

Know that you can open stores in other dollaripei countries on Amazon right from your desk, which means multiplying your earnings even further.

Now that you have a good understanding of this business, I'll explain exactly what steps you need to take.

- Product Research: Consider this as the most important step of the process, because only a careful market analysis will lead you to sell a successful product. You're looking for a product with low competition, that sells a lot, and even better if you can't find it easily in stores.

Another feature that is often underestimated is that of consumable products, which are bought several times even during the course of a month.

To search for products, I recommend you make use of a paid tool called JungleScout, which allows you to browse Amazon's categories and at the same time instantly know sales volumes, turnover and logistics rates.

- Product sourcing: The second step is to purchase the product in bulk, from China because it allows you to save a lot of money and the quality of the products is, contrary to common belief, really good. To search for the product I recommend you use Alibaba, an immense database of Chinese factories that are ready to produce and ship products that meet your needs and customizations. It would be better, before ordering a fair amount of items that meet at least the number of sales you project to make in a month, to buy a sample, and compare it with that of other factories.

- Product Shipping: Shipping can be by air, by sea.

The method you choose depends on the urgency with which you need the products, but also on the value of the products. What would be the point of shipping very inexpensive products by air, if shipping affects the final price more than the cost of the product itself? Almost all Chinese factories have a trusted shipping agent, so you can ask for a quote indicating your address.

They will ask you for an Incoterm, which is the code that indicates how far the seller's responsibility towards the shipment, and what I recommend and have been using for years is the DDU, which stands for "Delivery Duties Unpaid". Creation of the Product Page: In this phase you will have to create photos for your product, possibly with infographics and small text boxes to guide the customer in the choice. Next you will need to draft the title, bullet points, which is the description you see below the title, and the description at the bottom of the page.

- Shipping to Amazon's Warehouse: To ship products to Amazon's warehouse, simply convert your product page to "Managed by Amazon" and enter information about the packages you're going to explain, including size, weight, and number of units inside.

You'll be able to select UPS courier pickup at a very discounted rate. You'll also be able to arrange for the goods to arrive from China directly to Amazon's warehouse, but I recommend adopting this practice after you're confident in the quality of the goods you've purchased on Alibaba.

- Product Launch: Launching the product means making sure that organic sales start, i.e. without advertising. This phase is articulated differently depending on the competitiveness of the niche where you have entered. The more competitors there are, the harder it will be to get your product on the first page.

Amazon's algorithm makes sure that the best positioned products are the ones that sell the most, so you'll have to prove to Amazon that your product sells. To do this, you'll just need to do giveaways, which means giving away your product by creating discount codes from 90% and up and entering them into a platform called ViralLaunch, which will distribute them for you (right on EliteDealClub).

THE CON - But it's not all gold that glitters. Amazon's customers are very pretentious, and because of the A to Z guarantee, it's not hard for them to return the product and get a 100% return. That product, once opened, is no longer sellable as new and you'll almost be forced to have to throw it away. In addition, Amazon will not give you back logistics fees plus they will take a percentage of the commission on the final value which can be up to a maximum of $5. Another con is the competitiveness that is becoming more and more sanguine, resulting in less ability to sell many units per day. Last but not least is the issue of margins, which again due to competitiveness, commissions, and taxes, hardly reaches 30%.

This problem doesn't arise if you are good at differentiating yourself, selling something that you can't find in physical stores and that maybe you can't find on Alibaba, so you will dominate the market having a sort of exclusivity.

AFFILIATE PROGRAM

Thanks to the Amazon affiliate program you can earn a commission by promoting products that are for sale on Amazon, even if they are not offered for sale directly by you, but by third parties.

To make it simple for you, Amazon pays bloggers or people who run Facebook pages, Instagram or Telegram channels to bring people to buy the products on their site.

The affiliate system works like this:

1. You'll need to sign up for the Amazon affiliate portal;
2. Create and integrate affiliate links within your content on social or on your website;
3. When a user clicks on a product you have linked on your site, they will land on the Amazon sales page;

4. If this user eventually buys the product in question, Amazon will pay you a certain percentage of the sale price;

I imagine you'll be full of questions for me at this point, so I recommend you read the next few paragraphs carefully.

How does the system figure out that that person purchased because of me?

Amazon has developed an algorithm that allows you to create custom links for each person in your affiliate program, so that once they click on them, Amazon will be able to know "thanks to whom" that link was clicked and the sale was completed. Interesting, right?

At the end of each month you will be paid commissions after they exceed the $25 threshold, either via bank transfer or via the classic Amazon voucher.

Amazon's affiliate program has several important advantages for affiliates:

First, the commissions are satisfactory and depend from category to category, ranging from 3% to 10% of the cost of the product.

These commissions, once you reach the minimum payment threshold, will ALWAYS be paid to you. There is no way that one month you are not paid for whatever excuse.

Not to be underestimated is the interface of the affiliate program, really simple and intuitive: creating affiliate links has never been so easy.

Besides, you have access to a series of graphs that will allow you to keep an eye on your performance, the number of clicks and the very important conversion rate. Last but not least, you'll have access to the various possibilities Amazon offers to create sponsored content: banners, text links, HTML codes to embed in all sorts of ways.

COOKIES - A flaw in Amazon's Affiliate program are cookies, which for many online affiliate programs are stored, meaning that the system recognizes purchases made not only on the day the click occurs but up to 30 days later. Amazon doesn't use any cookies, it only credits you commissions on sales made within a single session, unless the customer places the item in the cart. In that case you will get your commissions if the purchase is completed within 90 days.

One silver lining, however, is that Amazon will credit you commissions for any purchase made within a single session (i.e. from the moment the user arrives on Amazon from one of your links), not just for the specific product you're sponsoring. What does this mean? It means that from the moment a customer lands on Amazon from your link and it occurs to them that they need to purchase any other item, you'll collect your percentage.

Another factor of Amazon that is definitely in our favor is the recommendation engine, which is the one that suggests related products to buyers that they can add to their cart. All commissions from products purchased in the same session will be recognized to you. Among the recommended products will also come out all those items that the customer has previously viewed, but has not yet purchased for whatever reason, and therefore most likely still needs.

After this quick introduction, here's the strategy for getting started with Amazon's affiliate program.

HOW TO FIND THE RIGHT NICHE - The niche you will need to fit into first of all should not be saturated, basically there should not be too many people who are sponsoring the same products, unless you feel they are working poorly and you can improve as you feel. Equally important is to search for a product that is highly searched on both Amazon and Google, 90% will always be purchased on Amazon.

Regarding search volumes on Amazon, I recommend using a very powerful tool called Helium10, which is the only one that has access to Amazon's search database.

Just enter the keyword you're interested in into the "Magnet" tool and you'll be able to compare the number of monthly searches with all the product searches you can think of. Similarly, you can check searches on Google's search engine by going to

Google Trends, which will also extrapolate data on the geographic location of those searching for that exact combination of words, also dividing them by region.

Logically leave out seasonal products, which will not bring you returns throughout the year but only for a few months. Instead, look for a niche with many reviews, obviously positive and with an average of at least 4 and a half stars, so that you can entice a potential buyer to convert. This way, he will be able to dissolve his last doubts and convince himself.

HOW TO CREATE CONTENT - Before you start creating content and sponsoring products in the Amazon catalog, you have to decide what format to follow. I'll propose several to give you some good ideas in mind, you'll be the one to forge your own strategy and determine which one works best. The model that I find most useful is a comparison between products in various situations of use.

Let's say you want to create a site to talk about soccer cleats. You could dedicate a section to shoes for the natural grass field, a section for those suitable for the synthetic turf field, one for soccer cleats, and so on. In each of these categories, show the pros and cons of each shoe, indicating the best one for each eventuality of use.

Another format is definitely that of the reviews, in practice you will have to tell your personal experience of products that you have personally tried, making a thorough analysis and not biased, indicating the reasons why a person should buy or not. This is a very useful solution for all those expensive product niches, which the average buyer prefers to know in detail first, doing a market research by searching on Google and will land on your site to get useful information.

Another idea is Aranzulla-style, on whose blog he suggests the product to solve a certain problem that arises during daily life. Take a tour of his site to get an idea, all the products he proposes are sold on Amazon and are sponsored links.

Other formats that I recommend are the cheaper products, or under a certain threshold of cost, or the even more creative videos on Youtube with the test of the product and the vision of the product in all its angles, which guides a lot of the purchase.

The icing on the cake are the Bestseller products, which can be of great interest to "lazy" buyers, who rely on the choices already made by thousands of customers who have purchased before him or her.

WEBSITE CREATION - Starting from 0, you have to buy a domain, and consider to buy a dry keyword domain, that is one that contains the keywords you are most interested in. If your niche is electronic cigarettes, buying the domain www.miglioresigarettaelettronica.it will be a good business card.

Both to buy the domain and to give it a structure, I recommend Aruba, which will provide the site with Wordpress pre-installed.

You'll be able to install the theme you prefer for your blog, and install a myriad of useful plugins like the Associates Link Builder, allows you to search for products in the Amazon catalog, access pricing and availability information in real time, and easily create links in your posts to products on Amazon.

Creating articles from the Wordpress dashboard is so simple that it's useless for me to explain it to you, but a key piece of advice I feel like giving you in the site building phase is to not put distractions in your pages, making the Amazon banner less visible and therefore less clicked.

At this point, however, your site still does not appear on Google, in fact you will have to report it to the search engine. Open the https://bit.ly/2VebGQP , enter the link to your site and the system will generate a code to insert in your blog. Then visit your website, and from the top bar of Wordpress click on Customize>Widget>Select Footer>Custom HTML and paste the string that was generated earlier. After a few days, your blog will be properly indexed in the Google search results!

To sponsor affiliate links or not?

Even I used to always wonder in the beginning whether or not I should create ad campaigns to bring traffic to my sponsored links, through Facebook and Instagram ADS, for example. The answer I now feel like giving is NO, 90% of the time it's just not worth it.

Unfortunately, the conversion rate of advertising is very low, precisely because the frequent users of social networks, are not very likely to leave the App, switch to the Browser and even worse to buy and kick money out of the wallet. At the limit they will open the link, make you spend money, and go back to the Facebook Homepage.

My NO to sponsored content is not a law, so it's worth it to try it and see how much margin you have after a conversion, and then let the whole mechanism go automatically, almost like a money machine, checking it from time to time.

To see if your selected audience is of good quality, i.e. well-targeted, you'll need to go and check the Facebook ADS relevance score that goes from 0 to 10, to see if your audience is interested in your link. If not, edit your demographic and interest information.

HOW TO OPEN AN ACCOUNT - From the homepage of www.programma-affiliazione.amazon.it click on the "Sign Up for Free" button, sign in with your Amazon customer account and confirm the primary contact person's information. After that you will have to list all the sites on which you will place sponsored content, such as Facebook pages or Blogs. Next, the system will ask you to create an affiliateID. After answering a series of personal questions, you will have successfully completed the registration.

HOW TO CREATE LINKS - You've found the product you want to sponsor, now you just need to create the link with your affiliate ID. It's very easy, you just need to be logged in with the account registered to the affiliate program and open the Amazon page of the item you want to sponsor. Under the address bar you will see that another bar has appeared, from which you can select the text link, which is a short Url that you can embed in the text or paste in a post on Facebook, or you can create real Html codes with the image of the product you are sponsoring.

In this case you can even select if you want the Amazon page to open in a new browser tab, which I highly recommend. People hate going back to the site where they were previously.

PROMOTIONS - Every month Amazon offers a series of really interesting promotions to promote its services. For example, if you sponsor the link to take advantage of the free month of Prime and a person uses it, you'll earn $1, while sponsoring Kindle Unlimited will earn $3 for each subscription signed up because of you. Check out this section and earn extra!

AFFILIATE PROGRAM COMMISSIONS

- TV, Smartphones and mobiles = 1%

- Computers, electronics, video games, photos and cameras, gift certificates = 3%

- Home, furniture, books, music, musical instruments, cooking, toys, DIY = 5%

- Sports and leisure, health and personal care, office products, early childhood, pet products, cars and motorcycles, garden, beauty, food = 7%

- Handmade = 10%

- Clothing, shoes, jewelry, luggage = 10%.

- All other products in categories not mentioned above = 3%.

KINDLE DIRECT PUBLISHING

How many times have you thought about writing a book and publishing it? Unfortunately, the approval of a text by a publishing house is very difficult, and if they accept anyway, your revenues will be really reduced to a minimum, basically it will all go into their pockets.

Fortunately, today there are more and more people approaching the world of Self Publishing who have discovered that it is possible to publish a book on Amazon for free.

Kindle Direct Publishing, in fact, offers the ability for authors to publish and distribute their books without going through a traditional publisher.

Authors can choose to participate in Kindle Direct Publishing Select, which automatically places the book among Kindle Unlimited titles.

Compensation for authors is determined, in addition to the number of units sold, by the number of pages read by Kindle Unlimited subscribers and Prime members who, among other things, can use the Kindle Owner's Lending Library service.

Among the strengths of the platform there are the possibility to launch the book on the market in less than 48 hours, the possibility to earn up to 70% royalties on sales and a small amount for each page read thanks to Kindle Unlimited, the possibility to have an always updated and transparent report on the revenues, as well as the excellent possibility to change at any time and at will the price and the description of the book in the Amazon page.

If you should notice spelling mistakes or a word you don't like, it won't be complicated to modify the content of the book and want to integrate something new.

The possibility of Kindle Direct Publishing is to publish both the digital and the paper version and keep them on the same product page, so a customer can choose whether to buy the digital or the physical version.

Another knot to consider: the author, although giving up a non-exclusive right to distribute their digital books, can join a program, KDP Select, which entails a commitment to make the digital version of the book available only through KDP and no other service, thus ensuring Amazon an exclusive.

AUTHOR CENTRAL - Author Central gives each KDP independent author the ability to create and customize their own profile, including a biography, photographs, videos and event dates. This is a great marketing tool that allows you to "cross sell", make your work better known and allows your books to be better positioned. also allows your books to be better positioned in search results.

THE CON - After so many pros, it behooves me to present the cons as well. KDP's advertising services are only active Amazon.com, which doesn't allow you to make your book more visible starting immediately. That doesn't take away from the fact that you will be able to do Advertising on Facebook or other sites to generate clicks and consequently conversions.

Another drawback is that it will not be possible for those who publish with KDP to organize presentations in bookstores, because bookstores sell publishers' books and you are outside the classic distribution circuit precisely because you are an independent author. Last but not least, you won't be able to participate with your book in literary contests, because the ISBN code you will be assigned belongs to Amazon, which is not a publisher but a sales platform.

Well, now that you have a complete overview of KDP, I'll walk you through how to get started and publish your first book for free and start billing from day one.

WHAT TO WRITE? - Writing what's on your mind is essentially what a book author does, maybe a novel or a manual, but this kind of approach won't get you to sell many units with confidence and consistency over time. That's because you have to go and see what the market is looking for but not finding on the Internet and particularly on Amazon, or put it down to the fact that the books there are on a specific topic are really scarce, which you can easily see from the reviews, only then is it worth entering.

For this reason we need to go and see the books that sell the most on Amazon, to this we will need a very useful tool called KDSpy. It is an extension for Chrome, so it works automatically while you browse the pages of Amazon, going to list the categories where there are the best ebooks by sales performance.

KDSpy will automatically search, in addition to our search, other more specific long tail keywords on which we will then have less competition.

We see that, for each search key, KDSpy reports the number of competitors and a traffic light that indicates how fierce the competition is.

Once all the data is collected, Kindle Spy can also extrapolate the recurring terms within the best-selling titles. This is a big help, not only in choosing what to write about, but more importantly in deciding what title to give your manuscript so that it will stand out in users' search results.

THE CHOICE OF NICHE- What I recommend is not to start from a main niche, but to dig deep to find minor niches that do not even have competition, but that ensure good results over time and still deal with interesting topics.

Amazon gives you the ability to create multiple identities, for example you can use your real to create books in the niche where you are more experienced, and different names for all the other niches. Keep in mind that it's always best to allocate a pen name to a specific niche until you dominate it with your books.

So using that pen name you'll start writing ebooks about a niche, but starting with the sub-niches, and slowly moving up, just to dominate that market. This way Amazon will see us as industry experts, and move our books up the search rankings.

REGISTRATION - To sign up, simply log in to KDP with your Amazon account credentials, then complete all the required information stating that you are not a U.S. citizen, enter your social security number and the iban to which the money from your books will be directed.

BOOK PREPARATION - To format your book in the Kindle format, I recommend using the Kindle Create PC software, which allows you to format the ebook version for the devices Amazon supports.

When you're done, the program will export a file in a special format that you only have to upload to the site.

It's a different matter for the paper version, which you'll have to provide to KDP in PDF format. Amazon supports several cages (paper sizes), but not all of those found in writing programs. Obviously within the book you will not be able to use photos you don't own downloaded from the internet, unless you buy them from Stock Photo sites, although there are databases of photos for free commercial use.

THE COVER - As for the cover, the cover of the Ebook format doesn't have to meet any particular requirements, so you can create it yourself even if you don't have graphic skills on sites like Canva.

As for the paper version, you'll have to be much more precise also because of the presence of the ISBN code that the system will insert automatically.

For this reason, I suggest you to contact a Freelancer graphic designer on Fiverr, who will prepare for you, for about 20$, the cover for the Kindle version and the cover for the paper version.

BOOK INSERT - Now that you have everything ready, you are ready to publish your first book. Fill out all of this information: Title, Subtitle, Author, Description (you can use html), publishing rights (i.e., whether you own the rights to offer this book for sale), the keywords most relevant to your book, and categories. At this point you will have to decide if you want to use DRM or Digital Rights Management, a technology that prevents unauthorized distribution of your book's Kindle files. Upload the book file and the cover file, then select the territories where you own the publishing rights.

Then select the cost of the MatchBook, i.e. the cost that the customer who buys the paper version has to pay to download the digital version as well.

THE ROYALTIES PLAN - At the time of publishing the book, either in the paper or digital version, you will have to decide on your royalties plan.

For the digital version, there is the 35% royalty plan and the 70% royalty plan. This means that if you sell an ebook, you will earn either 35% or 70% on the price of the book minus the cost of shipping the book (yes you heard me right, shipping an ebook), which amounts to $0.12 per megabyte of the file.

By choosing the 70% royalty plan you'll be tied to a number of constraints, such as setting the price between $2.99 and $9.99, and paying delivery costs. In this case you will be forced to subscribe your book to Kindle Unlimited, which is the service that allows subscribers to read books by paying only $10 per month. In addition, you'll have to participate in the Kindle Leading Program, which is a 14-day ebook lending service from the initial buyer to other readers, with no financial return to the author.

If you choose the 30% royalty plan you can choose any price between $0.99 and $215 and you won't pay delivery costs.

THE BOOK LAUNCH - Well, 24-48 hours after uploading, your book is finally online. To launch your book and get the first page sales flywheel going, it's not very difficult.

First, you'll need social proof - reviews from people who have purchased your book and are satisfied with it - to entice a potential buyer into thinking they won't regret paying for your book.

5-6 should be enough at first, and to get them just ask acquaintances to whom you have never been directly connected, such as in the same Wi-Fi connection, or who live in the same city as you. Try to cadence the publication of these reviews, having one written every 2 days so as not to arouse suspicion.

At this point you will need to pitch your book for a certain keyword, for example if you have written a romance novel, you will need to pitch your book with this keyword in order to push your book and get it all the way to the first page. For this purpose, we will need to create a free promotion of the digital version of your book, lasting up to 5 days. During this time, you will need to get as many people as possible to download your book, either by having them search for "romance novel", or by sending them a Super-Url, which is a link that contains the keyword you are interested in. Only in this way you will "trick" the Amazon algorithm and get your book positioned before all your competitors.

To create the Super-Url search for: "Gems Helium10", connect to the site and go under "7- 2 STEP URL VIA FIELD ASIN", enter the keyword and the ASIN of your book (which is an 8-digit code that you find in the details of your book on the sales page). The link you get is for Amazon.com, so you need to substitute ".it" for

".com" and the Super-Url will be ready. To send it to your friends I recommend shortening it using the Bitly site.

After 5 days of promotion check how you are doing and if your book is indexed better in search results, otherwise repeat this promotion for another 5 days, also sponsoring in Facebook groups your new book in free promotion that will arouse the curiosity of potential readers.

Once your book is launched, you'll see how the sales will start coming in and you'll be raking in money without doing a damn thing. You've built an asset from nothing to put on your personal balance sheet, so you're ready to write another book and double down, and then again and again. To collect this money, unfortunately, the timeline is a bit long. Royalties will only be credited to you if you exceeded the $100 threshold in the month, otherwise they will be added to the following month's royalties. Royalties for the month will be paid to you 60 days after the end of the month, so you will receive your earnings for all of January at the end of March.

PHANTOM WRITERS - If you don't feel able to write a book because you may not have the imagination or time, you could use a ghost writer. A ghost writer is a person who writes a book for you and in exchange for money will send you the file that you can publish under your name and earn all the royalties. You can find a person to write a book for you on Fiverr, or try asking friends who are knowledgeable in an interesting niche and are willing to help you.

AMAZON VENDOR PROGRAM

With the Amazon Vendor Central program, you go from being a simple seller on Amazon to being an Amazon vendor, which means you start selling products marked "Sold and Shipped by Amazon", which is a major advantage over someone who sells with FBA and has "Sold by Tweedledum and Shipped by Amazon" on their products. Basically, with the Vendor program, in addition to the trust of shipping through Amazon, there is the fact that the goodness of the product is certified by Amazon itself.

Unfortunately, this is an invite-only program, it's not open to everyone who manufactures a product line (or brands it by doing private label by importing it from China) and it doesn't fit within some of Amazon's parameters. However, you will be bound to accept the sale price that Amazon imposes on you, which minimizes your margins as the site's intent is to get competitive prices from its suppliers and also reduce its own margins by focusing on quantity.

Owning a registered trademark, you will be able to access the A+ contents, that is the descriptions with images and comparative tables, which will allow you to sell to the final customer the product with the technical features and functionalities that most satisfy him, allowing you to do cross selling (i.e. I buy item A, and

I also buy item B). Another advantage is the video that you can add to the product page, which is no small thing, and the creation of your brand page (https://amzn.to/2U8yAcl is the brand page of Samsung, really well built).

With the Vendor program all you have to do is sell large pallets of items to Amazon and ship the inventory to the warehouses. Amazon handles the inventory and handles the logistics, returns and customer service entirely. You'll be relying on the world's largest ecommerce site to sell products for you in all marketplaces, guaranteeing you really big reorders if the product is quality and sells well.

Consider that products sold by Amazon itself are displayed first in the search results, getting incredible visibility, as the same possibility to access the services "Prime Now", "Amazon Pantry" or "Subscribe and Save" will increase the number of customers.

Another plus point is the marketing services, implemented over the possibilities that FBA's SellerCentral gives you. You'll have access to "Amazon Vine", which is the only way to get reviews in compliance with Amazon's regulations. Basically you can send your products for free to testers selected by Amazon, who will have to write an honest review of your product, highlighting its merits and defects, in short, not biased and necessarily 5 stars.

One small drawback is that Amazon's payment times are quite slow, they could last up to 90 days, so forget about cash flow.

As I said at the beginning, if you're not invited you won't be able to take part, so you should consider the Vendor Express sales option, which I'll explain in the next chapter.

VENDOR EXPRESS PROGRAM

Vendor Express is very similar to Vendor Central, you will always have to own a brand, but you won't need to be invited.

Vendor Express is a great way for a young/small business to get into wholesale and potentially grow. However, you won't have access to A+ pages (which are estimated to convert 10-15% more than text-only pages), and Amazon Vine.

What's unique about this sales program is that you'll be able to take care of the delivery to the end customer yourself, and the icing on the cake is that Amazon will provide you with prepaid shipping labels with their trusted courier, who will pick up the package directly at your warehouse.

However, if you want to change even one comma in your product page because you think something is wrong, or maybe you have been unpersuasive to induce the purchase, you'll have to be afraid of the biblical time, since it will be an Amazon employee to check and in case approve. On SellerCentral it only takes 15 minutes to do all this and the changes will be online, but logically Amazon does it to protect itself and avoid that you describe the product as not being so.

In addition, participating in the Vendor or Vendor Express program does not assure you of having margins because Amazon will only make an estimate with respect to what are the prices of competitors, it does not care about your real production costs. No one is forcing you to take it, of course, but it's worth a try.

Another factor to be careful about is the sales policy, you'll have to establish a minimum sale price on Amazon that doesn't put your offline retailers (as well as online ones, if you have any) in a war footing, because of the competitiveness of Amazon's service that is grabbing new customers day after day.

AMAZON HANDMADE

Handmade is a category of Amazon entirely dedicated to handmade products. To become part of it you must be eligible, your request will be reviewed by the staff after completing an online form.

You will be asked for several pieces of information about your craft, such as the production process, including photos and your place of business. Amazon's staff will carefully check if the type of products you produce is entirely handmade (and of course with light production means such as a hot glue gun), or if you make use of kits, and if so your request will be rejected.

Handmade is still in its beta phase, which is why there are no upfront costs or subscriptions, you will "only" pay 12% when you have made a sale. You will be able to access Amazon's logistics services and sell in all of the dollaripei marketplaces at the same time.

Another possibility that Amazon Handmade gives you is to be able to provide customizations to products, making customers pay for them with surcharges.

The categories within Handmade are several: Jewelry, Bags and Accessories, Home Decor, Art, Cooking and Dining, Childhood, Games and Toys, Stationery, and Beauty.

After this introduction to the service, you're almost ready to sell your artifacts on Handmade.

HOW TO LIST ITEMS - The dashboard you'll have available to put your artifacts up for sale is the classic SellerCentral. From "Catalog" click on "Add Products" and select the category of the item. Fill in the information about the price, the measures and the customizations I mentioned before.

After that save and you will find the product in your inventory available for sale. Click on the top right on "Settings" and then "Shipping Settings" to create your shipping plan, selecting shipping types and their prices. To associate this shipping model with the products for sale, go to the inventory and from the drop-down menu next to the item price click on "Change Shipping Model" and select the new one.

You may decide to convert your listing in the FBA management, but I highly discourage it first of all because customers will not be able to select customizations, and secondly because the product would undergo too many steps and would be very easily damaged even by Amazon operators.

Next think about updating your craftsman showcase, inserting your personal information that might be of interest to a customer, including your featured products and don't forget to tell the story behind your productions, so the creative process.

DISCLAIMER

All trademarks and logos mentioned in this book belong to their rightful owners.

The author does not claim or represent any rights to these trademarks, which are mentioned for educational purposes only.

Day Trading After the Pandemic:

How to Achieve Super Performance in 2021

BOOK 3

All rights reserved

DISCLAIMER:

This manual aims to provide the reader with a complete expositive picture of the subject matter of this manual, Online Trading. The information contained herein is verified according to scientific studies, however the author is not responsible for how the reader applies the acquired information. For any doubts the reader can refer to a specialist in the field.

Table of Contents

Introduction

I n the last few years it has become more and more common to hear about online trading: and around this definition has been generated an aura of mystery, as if this financial instrument could be a sort of panacea, able to make anyone rich quickly, even starting with a small capital, or a sort of legalized "scam", a dangerous world populated by shady individuals (traders, in fact) from which to keep a distance.

In fact, although more complex, the definition in Italian is certainly the one that best renders the meaning of online trading: "negotiation" means an activity of purchase and sale (precisely the one carried out by the trader, in the hope of earning on the price difference); "telematics" because online trading takes place only with the use of computer systems that remotely communicate with each other and transfer data; "financial securities" because online trading deals only with a single "product" or "commodity", precisely financial securities.

So, the "commodity" that is traded in online trading is not a real good (like a pair of shoes or a batch of food). It is not even money, but securities that represent, for those who own them, the possession of something. A typical example of a financial security is the stock, that is that part of itself, or rather of its capital, which a company decides to sell to a person who thus becomes a shareholder of the company itself. Financial securities are many, some are very complex in nature, they are different and function and are regulated differently. They are completely dematerialized securities: there is no longer a sheet of paper attesting to the possession of a security, but every aspect of the "life" of a financial security is managed electronically.

Obviously, investing in financial securities represents a risk, especially because there is no exact science that allows you to determine the trend of the same: for this reason around the online trading have arisen a whole series of "urban legends", which tell, alternately, easy wealth and huge losses.

This book aims at clarifying the nature and functioning of online trading, examining its different aspects and paying special attention to those technical analysis tools and their parameters that allow to reduce the margin of uncertainty that is present in this type of activity.

In addition, among other aspects that will be examined, there will be the operational strategies with which to trade, the importance of trading volume and risk management, of paramount importance to avoid finding yourself in a short time without a capital to invest in online trading. The same attention will be given to the necessary instrumentation to do the best online trading, the choice of the online broker and the functioning of the platforms through which to trade.

Without forgetting the normative, regulatory and fiscal aspect of online trading, which includes an examination of the entities, both Italian and international, that work to protect the correct course of the financial market and therefore also the position of small traders and the fiscal aspects that must be taken into account when it is necessary to calculate the taxation to which the profits obtained through online trading are subjected.

The last part of the book will be dedicated to the importance of continuing education to become a good trader, the automated services that can be used in online trading and what are the most common (but also most dangerous) mistakes every trader can make.

A trader is not born, but it is certainly possible to become one, learning the characteristics of the tools you have at your disposal and discovering the "tricks" that govern the world of online trading.

Chapter 1

A Brief History of Online Trading

Online trading before the www: a market for a select few

As it often happens, it is impossible to fix a precise date for the birth of online trading: if it is true that its diffusion necessarily corresponds with the mass diffusion of data communication systems on the net, it is also true that the roots must be looked for definitely before the nineties.

In particular, the trading market already experienced an important growth between 1950 and 1960, thanks to a significant increase in the number of operators and the volume of exchanges related to currency operations, made possible by the birth of the TELEX system, perfect for making the activities carried out within the financial market simpler and faster.

But the exponential growth of trading can be seen from the eighties onwards, also thanks to the possibility of exchanging currency on the markets 24 hours a day, 7 days a week: in these years banks and brokers able to manage huge capitals (and therefore to face the expenses related to this kind of operations) became the protagonists of the trading world. We have to understand how during all these years the trading market was hardly accessible to the general public, given the need to commit significant capital and also given the characteristics with which the operations were carried out on the market: in fact, several operations had to be necessarily carried out in person and this involved a significant commitment of time and money.

The eighties: the net revolution arrives and the first generation of online brokers

The eighties represent not only one of the moments of greatest growth of the trading market, but also a real watershed: in particular we can consider 1982 the year in which the first generation of modern online brokers was born. In this year, three brokers (Max Ule & Co. Naico-Net and C.D. Andersons) created, independently of each other, systems for telematically negotiating financial securities, to which was connected a special software that had the function of analyzing data from the stock exchange.

This is an important step forward, so much so that two years later, in 1984, as many as 8000 brokers are offering a system of access for electronic trading of financial securities: as a result of this, the number of clients is also growing, reaching over

500,000. This rapid and almost uncontrolled growth also has its negative sides, because in the second half of the decade, cases of financial fraud linked to online trading multiplied. But the black year is 1987, when the "black monday" of all markets sends a large number of small and medium-sized financial companies into default, sending even the larger ones into crisis.

The second generation of online brokers and the impact of the world wide web: the birth of the third generation of brokers

From the ashes of the first generation of online brokers, a new generation of brokers was born, who found themselves, in the early nineties, facing a new revolution: that of the Internet. If at the beginning of the decade there were less than 10 sites active on the network (or rather the forerunners of modern sites), by 1993 there were more than 500 and by 1994 there were more than 10,000. Not all financial companies are ready to adapt to this epochal change and the umpteenth generational change occurs, with the arrival of the third generation of brokers, who carry out their activity through the web (among the pioneers of this era are Wall Street Investor Services and Securities APL).

In addition to growing exponentially, the spread of the net leads to the diffusion of online trading outside the borders of the United States: Europe and Asia also enter the world of next-generation trading and brokers

Chapter 2

The financial instruments of online trading

I n order to be able to trade online in the correct way, we cannot disregard the knowledge of the financial products that are negotiated through trading operations: these are very different instruments, which hide very different rules and mechanisms that make them suitable for particular and specific risk profiles. The theoretical knowledge of these instruments is therefore the starting point to operate in online trading.

A fairly cursory but overall correct breakdown of the financial instruments that can be traded can lead to the creation of a few broad categories:

- shares: securities that represent an equity stake in a company; bonds:

- securities that represent a debt stake in a company;

- derivative contracts or simply "derivatives": securities which in turn represent other securities or actual commodities;

- ETFs: securities that represent units of investment funds;

- cryptocurrencies: digital currencies

Actions

Shares are a tool that allows you to buy a part of the capital of a company: in most cases a company sells part of its capital to raise funds (which can be used to develop or to pay debts or even to acquire other companies). With the purchase of shares you become, to all intents and purposes, a shareholder of a company and therefore you acquire two different types of rights:

- Patrimonial rights: which represent the possibility of obtaining a profit, if the company itself obtains a profit, in the form of part of the profits;

- Administrative rights: Owning shares allows you to participate in the administration of the company (e.g. by exercising your right to vote at the company's general meeting).

The value of the shares of a given company depends on the overall value of the company itself, which can be influenced by various factors (such as the company's business performance or particular external events such as catastrophes, particular technological developments or the performance of a market sector).

In trading systems, stocks are divided into four main groups:

- European
- U.S.
- rest of the world.

Bonds

When we speak of bonds we refer to a security that represents a part (or quota) of a debt of the subject that issues the bond itself. This party, which may be a company, a bank, a state or a supranational body, takes on a debt towards the parties that purchase the bonds, undertaking to repay the capital within a set deadline and paying interest for the money received. The interest rate may be fixed, variable, composite, paid in several instalments or in a single payment.

Bonds are characterized by a nominal value, which corresponds to the capital repaid at maturity: during the period in which the bonds are listed, their actual value may be different from the nominal value, always depending on the perception of value and on the economic situation of the issuer (in particular with regard to its ability to honour debts).

In online trading the gain depends on the difference between the purchase price and the sale price and any interest received.

Derivative securities

When we talk about derivatives, we must always remember that we are entering the world of "creative finance": in fact, these are financial instruments of a complex nature, which are divided into different subcategories, all of which in turn have different technical characteristics. A common point among derivative securities is that they are securities with no intrinsic value: if, for example, a share has a value because it represents the capital share of a company, the derivative security bases its value on other financial products or even on goods, to whose price variations the derivative securities can be linked. The security or commodity to which the derivative is linked is also called the "underlying".

This type of contract originates from commodity exchanges (i.e., those markets where commodities such as livestock, various minerals or grain are traded), with the function of setting a determined price for those goods that are physically delivered at a later time than the purchase (the harvest of grain or oranges, for example) and to avoid the physical movement of goods between different parties, when different buying and selling operations occur.

Some derivatives require the underlying asset to be delivered at the expiration of the contract: in online trading, derivative securities are usually sold prior to expiration, precisely to avoid the step of physical delivery of the commodity, and almost all online brokers provide that derivative positions are closed ex officio prior to expiration if they provide for physical delivery of the commodity.

You can think of a derivative as a bet: in fact, with this instrument you try to predict what the trend of a certain type of price will be.

CFD

CFDs (Contracts for Difference) are a particular type of derivative contract: their value is based on the price changes of the financial asset that represents the underlying, for example the exchange rate between two currencies or the price of a stock. In this case, a CFD might be linked to the value of the shares of a particular company, and the value of the derivative is derived from changes in the value of the shares.

Options

Options are also a type of derivative contract that does not provide for an obligation, but rather a "possibility" (option) to sell (call option) or buy (put option) an underlying asset at a certain date and at a certain price.

Thus, the elements underlying an option contract are:

- A right (not an obligation) to buy or sell a particular underlying asset;
- the underlying asset: which is the object of the option and can be a commodity, an interest rate or a security;

- the strike price: the price predetermined in the contract at which it can be bought or sold;
- the date: which fixes the expiry date within which the option can be exercised;
- the premium: i.e. the cost paid for the option contract.

Binary Options

Like the classic option, the binary option is a derivative instrument that allows you to trade an underlying asset (sell or buy) at a specific price and at a specific expiry time. However, the binary option offers only two possible alternatives: whether or not a certain prediction will occur in relation to the price development of the underlying asset. If the prediction occurs, you receive a premium (already determined by the contract), otherwise you lose the invested capital.

An example of a binary option can be one that predicts that the price of a certain underlying asset will increase over a certain period of time (there are binary options that also predict very short intervals).

Among the binary options should be remembered:

- interval options: which involve guessing the price interval in which the underlying asset will be at the expiration of the option;
- touch options: which involve guessing whether the underlying will reach a certain value in a given time interval.

ETF

ETFs (Exchange Traded Funds) are mutual funds listed on the stock exchange. Their management is completely passive, because they simply replicate the performance of an index (the benchmark).

Purchases of ETFs do not require a broker and can be made directly on the stock exchange and the quotation of these securities changes during the course of a day (as happens with shares). Furthermore, ETFs are characterized by a spread that is equal to the difference between the price that intermediaries propose for the purchase (lower) and that proposed for the sale (higher).

ETC

ETCs (Exchange Traded Commodities) are derivative securities that a party issues linking them to an investment made directly in commodities or in derivatives linked to commodities. These are securities that are listed on the stock exchange (like shares) and have a passive management (which follows the trend of a benchmark).

There are two markets on which ETCs are listed:

- primary market: only authorized brokers operate on this market, it offers the possibility of buying and selling ETCs on a daily basis, following the official value of the security;

- secondary market: all investors operate in this market and it is a quotation market (the price of the security is determined on the basis of the purchase and sale proposals at different times).

ETN

ETNs (Exchange Traded Notes) are derivative securities that an entity issues by linking them to an investment made in an underlying that is not a commodity or to a derivative linked to this underlying. These securities are listed on the stock exchange and are characterized by passive management (which faithfully follows the trend of an index or benchmark).

These securities are traded on two different markets and with different procedures: the primary market is reserved for authorized parties, the secondary market provides free access for all investors.

Futures

The future is a derivative instrument consisting of a contract, signed between buyer and seller, which obliges the parties to sell and buy a certain number of underlyings (raw materials or other commodities) or securities, financial index or currency. The exchange takes place at a price already fixed in the contract and on a predetermined date. It is an instrument that is very popular in the field of online trading.

It is a symmetrical contract, whereby both parties assume an obligation to the counterparty, and a standard contract, which is traded on regulated markets, whereby the parties cannot change its terms (such as duration, price, denomination or underlying asset).

This is a contract created as a risk hedging instrument, to protect companies that have to purchase large quantities of certain goods, which by using this type of contract are protected from upward price fluctuations of the prices of the raw materials themselves.

In online trading, the future has a typically speculative use: the trader has no interest in closing the contract and obtaining the underlying asset, but speculates on the increase and decrease in value of the asset itself, which directly affects the value of the future.

This is a particularly delicate and complex instrument, the correct use of which is supervised by an independent authority: in Italy, this role is covered by the Cassa di Compensazione e Garanzia (CCG), whose task is to safeguard the deposits that the parties to futures contracts must pay to guarantee their solvency.

Certificate

If the future is a contract, the certificate is instead a real security which is issued by a credit institution and which is also called "securitized derivative". It is therefore a derivative that is composed of several other derivatives, in particular options, and allows the implementation of very articulated investment strategies.

This instrument does not pay dividends or management costs, but is subject to the risk of bankruptcy of the issuer (resulting in loss of principal).

Certificates are divided into two main categories:

- leveraged;
- without leverage (which replicate the performance of the underlying).

As far as invested capital goes, it can be:

- unprotected;
- partially protected (with guaranteed repayment at maturity of a portion of the nominal principal);
- fully protected (thus guaranteeing full repayment at maturity of the nominal value).

Covered Warrants

Covered Warrants (CW) are securities that can be issued by credit institutions: this is a securitized derivative, which provides the buyer with the option to buy or sell the underlying at a predetermined price and date. CWs are distinguished into:

- call: when they invest in the rise in the price of the underlying asset;

- put: when they invest in the fall in the price of the underlying asset.

Cryptocurrencies

Cryptocurrencies represent one of the most important innovations born from the meeting of finance and advanced technology: they are a particular form of digital currencies that are managed through complex cryptographic systems (in particular blockchain technology and distributed databases). Therefore, they are currencies with completely decentralized management: they do not depend on any national or supranational entity.

This is an absolutely new financial asset that is characterized by wide volatility, with prices rising and falling very quickly. The most well-known cryptocurrencies are Bitcoin and Ethereum. Some brokers offer the possibility to trade cryptocurrencies.

Chapter 3

What is speculation?

When we talk about speculation we tend to give a negative meaning to this term: in reality, it is enough to know its origin to understand that the reality is very different. Because "speculation" derives from "specula", term with which the ancient Romans indicated the lookout, that is the one who controlled and protected the other soldiers. For this reason, the speculator can be defined as a careful observer of reality, who, based on his observations and predictions, makes decisions.

And speaking of speculation in online trading, it becomes evident that any negative meaning has disappeared: in fact, the speculator simply becomes a person who makes investments, accepting the risks associated with them. In particular, speculation aims to gain through price fluctuations that affect financial instruments.

As far as the "time factor" is concerned, which is often decisive in the field of speculation, in online trading the intervals are short or even very short (typical is the case of binary options).

Speculation can be carried out "upwards" (i.e. buying a security with the hope of reselling it in the future at a higher price) or "downwards" (i.e. selling a security in anticipation of a fall in its price).

Short speculation

There is also a particular type of speculation that is carried out only through the buying and selling of financial instruments: short speculation. The premise of this type of speculation is that the trader does not own the security or asset on which he intends to speculate, so he must borrow (normally from a credit institution or an intermediary) these instruments. In exchange for this loan it is necessary to pay an interest (which becomes more and more onerous as time passes, for this reason speculations must be carried out in short intervals).

The typical example of short speculation is that carried out downwards: you sell securities in the hope that their price will fall, and then buy them back at a lower price (in this way, in addition to obtaining a profit, you also get the interest to be paid to the bank). In the event of a mistake on the speculation, it becomes necessary to buy the securities at a higher price and bear the inevitable losses.

Chapter 4

Fundamental and Technical Analysis

After having seen the birth and evolution of online trading and having understood which are the instruments through which you can operate, the moment has come to "take the field" and face the market: attention, this doesn't mean to throw ourselves headlong in the investments on the net, but to continue our preparation going to know those that are considered the two fundamental methods to face the market, that is the fundamental analysis and the technical analysis.

Fundamental analysis: principles and limits

The objective of fundamental analysis is to guess the "right" price of a security, a currency, a commodity or an index, and to achieve this result it studies a whole series of data (for example, data emerging from the balance sheets of a company, data of the economic dynamics of a given sector, data relating to the evolution of interest rates in a given period, data relating to the balance of payments in a given country).

The route taken in fundamental analysis is to start from the cause in order to predict the effect, in this case the trend of the price of a particular security or other financial instrument: according to this type of analysis, when the price of a particular security or index is lower than the theoretical price derived from fundamental analysis, it is time to buy, and when the price reaches the theoretical maximum, always deduced through analysis, it is time to sell.

This type of analysis has many limitations: in fact, it is very difficult to correctly evaluate all the factors that may come into play in the determination of a price, especially if you do not have effective models related to the economy. In addition, it is a "slow" type of analysis: often fundamental analysis is not able to able to keep up with the rapid changes occurring on the market, therefore the real risk is to terminate the analysis procedure and thus determine a theoretical price when the price movement itself is over.

And this is not even the most serious problem: in fact, this type of analysis is based on the assumption that the market moves in the most rational and efficient way possible, linking price variations only to concrete and ascertained events and situations. It's a pity that reality is very different: very often it's the rumors, the chatters, even the emotions that determine the market variations in the short and very short period. This means that, especially for those who trade online, considering that speculation in this field occurs in very short intervals, fundamental analysis may not be a completely adequate tool.

Fundamental analysis remains instead a useful tool to interpret movements in the long term (we are talking about at least some months or even years). For a trader it is however always important to know the evolution of fundamental data during a relatively short period, such as the one included in a week: in particular, if the market is waiting for particularly important data, which can change in a marked way certain situations, it is necessary to be prepared.

As far as the practical management of the fundamental analysis is concerned, a basic principle must always be kept in mind, that is that the market always tends to "move in advance": often, when positive data are made public, for example related to the trend of the balance sheet of a company, the stock itself tends to go down, because its price had previously risen just waiting for these data. The opposite often happens when negative data are made public, so at the moment of publication there is a rebound of the stock upwards.

This principle is well expressed in the phrase "Buy on rumors, sell on facts", which indicates to buy when positive expectations start to circulate, while the time to sell is when these expectations become real and are made known to the public.

Technical Analysis

Very different is instead the approach foreseen by technical analysis: in fact, this type of analysis starts from the assumption that it is impossible to identify the "right" price of a security, of an index or of any other financial instrument. Moreover, the market does not behave rationally and efficiently in its variations, which are instead strongly influenced by elements that are difficult to predict, such as fear or hope, behaviors typical of human beings who are those who make up the financial market.

Therefore, at the base of technical analysis there is not the research of "why" a particular price fluctuation occurs or of a particular logic behind these fluctuations: there is instead a different objective, which is to be "in the right place at the right time", in order to maximize gains and decrease losses. Technical analysis has the objective of identifying those levels of entry and exit from a market that are interesting from the point of view of the risk-benefit ratio.

From this we can deduce how the two types of analysis, which could often produce different and contrasting results, are instead useful if exploited in a complementary way. In fact the fundamental analysis has the function to give indications on all profitable investments in the long run, while the technical analysis indicates when is the best moment to enter in a determined market and a price objective in which to exit from the market, possibly with a "take profit" or in some cases with a "stop-loss".

Considering the time intervals in which you operate in online trading, the tool to use is always and only that of technical analysis.

The fundamental principles of technical analysis

As much as technical analysis eschews the search for the right price and the causes of fluctuations, it is a tool that is based on three fundamental principles:

- Fundamentals are found within the price;

- market movement follows trends;

- history tends to repeat itself. Let's look at these three principles in detail.

Fundamentals are found within the price

According to this principle, the prices of a financial instrument, which are the result of the encounter between supply and demand, are the mirror in which all available information on that instrument is reflected, even that which is known to a limited number of people.

Market movement follows trends

Market movements are never completely random, but follow a trend (which can be upward, downward or sideways). The objective of a trader must be to understand what trend is in place and enter the market in order to exploit it, riding the trend in place to maximize gains.

History tends to repeat itself

The fact that some situations tend to repeat cyclically on financial markets is due to the fact that at the base of the markets there are human beings, who oscillate between the desire to gain and the fear of losing money: for this reason the study of the past can provide useful indications to understand the present and predict the future. With the analysis of historical graphs it is possible to identify patterns, for which, given a starting situation, a certain evolution is probable. Obviously the analysis does not have the objective to give always precise indications, but to supply some indications at operative level to manage complicated and potentially risky market situations.

Chapter 5

Technical Analysis in Online Trading

H aving understood what the theoretical foundations of technical analysis are, the next step is to understand how to apply it to online trading: we have seen how this type of analysis focuses mainly on the price dynamics of financial instruments and how, considering that history repeats itself on the market, through the study of the past it is possible to understand and anticipate the dynamics of the market itself.

Thanks to the use of technical analysis it is possible to identify the "levels" of entry and exit from a particular market and, based on these data, develop a trading project: because for the trader it is not important to "guess" the right price, but to be "in the right place at the right time" in order to maximize gains and minimize losses.

Technical analysis tools

In the attempt to predict the price fluctuation of a financial instrument (which can be a commodity, a security, an index or a currency), technical analysis offers a whole series of tools, more or less complex, that investors can use: in particular, very interesting is the Fibonacci analysis, a tool that is based on Dow's theory, according to which the market has the tendency to move in a predictable way, following precise patterns that tend to repeat themselves.

For this reason, in practice, technical analysis focuses on reading the patterns that can be drawn from the charts, always starting from the principle that price fluctuations that have occurred in the past have the tendency to repeat themselves in a cyclic way: leaving out all the aspects related to fundamental analysis, the trader's task is to focus the attention on price charts.

In the study of charts the objective is to identify a whole series of patterns already known: for example the so-called reversal figures, such as "Head & Shoulders" and "Double Maximum" and indicators, such as moving averages.

The trends and the theory of Dow

We have seen how one of the fundamentals of technical analysis is that markets do not move at random, but follow trends that a trader can identify. Charles Dow (creator of the Dow Jones stock index) is one of the theorists of market trends. Comparing the price trend with that of the tides, Dow had found analogies between the movements: the tide advances, retreats and moves further ahead, until it reaches a point where the process reverses and the market moves in the same way.

There are phases when the trend is increasing and phases when the trend is decreasing. Dow identifies three main types of trends:

- major trend: that lasts also years, similar to the tides;
- medium trend: that lasts some months, similar to the waves;
- minor trend: lasting a few weeks, similar to wave breakers.

And within different temporal horizons there are different trends: if we want to apply this technique to online trading, the major trend is the one resulting from the chart of the day, the medium trend is the hourly one and the minor trend is the one related to a chart of 5-minute intervals. A given trend line (uptrend or downtrend) is stronger the longer it lasts and lasts until the moment when there are no signs of exhaustion or reversal of the trend (for example, when the trend line "breaks", with a sudden fall).

If on a trading chart it is possible to identify a succession of more or less highs and lows, according to Dow's theory, we are in a bullish market, while if on a trading chart it is possible to identify a succession of decreasing highs and lows, according to Dow's theory, we are in a bearish market.

Be careful though, because the breaking of a trend, that is the reversal of the trends seen above, while marking the end of the itself, does not lead to an automatic reversal of the trend itself: in this phase it could in fact start a phase of "lateral" movement for the market, characterized by a low volume of exchanges, in which the trend "pauses", waiting for a new restart.

Identify trend changes with the Fibonacci method

To predict the behavior of trends one of the most used systems is the Fibonacci Tracking, based on an infinite sequence of numbers discovered by the Italian mathematician Fibonacci in the 13th century. In practice you start with two numbers, such as 1 and 2, which are added together to get the third number in the sequence and so it goes:

1-1-2-3-5-8-13-21-34-55-89-144

One of the characteristics of this sequence of numbers is that each individual digit is about 1.618 times larger than the digit that precedes it: and it is precisely this relationship that is used for the levels of the tracking patterns. To do this you take two points on a chart, an absolute minimum and an absolute maximum and divide them from top to bottom by the Fibonacci percentages (23.6%, 38.2%, 50%, 61.8% and 100%). In this way, levels are identified and it is at these levels, according to analysts, that price movements tend to reverse and therefore the change in trend occurs.

The percentages for identifying levels are obtained from the ratios between the numbers in the sequence:

- 61.8% by dividing one number in the sequence by the next number: 21/34 = 0.6176, also known as the Golden Ratio;

- 38.2% dividing one number in the sequence by the second number that follows it: 55/144 = 0.3819;

- 23.6% by dividing one number in the sequence by the third number that follows it: 13/55 = 0.2363.

The typical behavior of a price is to run through the 38.2% to 61.8% levels of the previous movement before continuing in the same trend: it is not possible to understand the reason why this happens, but these ratios play an important role in the market and traders use them to determine the critical points where a trend reverses.

Doji Candle

If the opening price and the closing price coincide, we are in front of a Doji candle: taken individually, a Doji candle only represents a situation for which neither those who bet on the rise, nor those who bet on the fall have been successful. This type of candle should be analyzed according to the orientation of the previous candle:

- after a rise a Doji candle signals that the buying trend starts to decrease;

- after a fall a Doji candle signals that the selling trend starts to decrease.

So the presence of a Doji candle is the signal of change in the trend: using candlestick analysis for traders it is possible to get important information about the trend of a particular market.

Mobile Averages

A moving average is an indicator that shows the average value of a financial instrument in a given time interval: it is used to eliminate the disturbance in the analysis that can be caused by random price fluctuations. To calculate a moving average we use historical values and data, such as :

- positive peaks
- negative peaks
- opening prices and closing
- volumes.

The most common moving averages are the simple moving average (SMA) and the exponential moving average (EMA): the main difference is given by the weight that in the calculation of the average is referred to the data of different periods. For example, the exponential moving average (EMA) considers with greater attention the most recent data, while the simple moving average (SMA) gives the same value to all data.

The time period over which to calculate a moving average can be long or short, ranging from minutes to years: the choice depends on the trend you are operating on, and you can choose as many time periods as you want.

The simple moving average is an arithmetic average, which is calculated by first calculating the closing prices of a given number of time periods and then dividing the sum by the same number of time periods.

The result you get is a positive or negative trend, which can provide a rough direction of market movement.

The exponential moving average (EMA) is a type of weighted moving average that gives more importance to the most recent data, being more responsive to price fluctuations than the simple moving average. This moving average can be used in online trading to find the optimal point to enter or exit the market, although it is a less accurate average in the long term.

Chapter 6
The Importance of Volumes

A separate chapter and a particular attention must be given to Volumes in the analysis for online trading. The importance of understanding and analyzing volumes depends mainly on the fact that these values are able to offer an overview of a market almost "in real time" and are based on data that can be considered "certain".

The Volumes represent the quantity of trades that are carried out with respect to a specific financial instrument (index, security, currency, commodity) in a given time interval. The analysis of Volumes is based on data that can be interpreted in a quite simple way, moreover it is an analysis that takes place in real time (unlike moving averages): for this reason, a complete analysis in the field of online trading cannot not take volumes into consideration.

To calculate volumes, you must add up the number of contracts for a given asset traded in a time frame, regardless of the number of trades and the number of parties involved in the trades.

How to use values in online trading

The indications furnished from the volumes are enough simple to decipher, can be more complicated to estimate these operations in the within of a wider analysis that aims to define a strategy of trading. In particular the absolute value of the values is an indication not completely useful in this sense, while an importance decidedly greater goes attributed to the relationship between volumes and prices. Three scenarios can be verified that can be defined "typical":

Rising volumes and rising prices: considering that volumes represent the amount of transactions carried out on a given asset, at a historical level, when the price rises, there is also an increase in volumes. This is an axiom that proves to be valid especially in the equity field. Therefore, in the presence of both of these conditions, a stock can be expected to be in an uptrend: however, if the value of volumes does not appear sufficiently robust, this trend is not consolidated and the price of the stock could fall quickly;

Low volumes and prices in descent: what has been said above cannot be applied in a specular way when the prices tend to the decrease. It is not necessary to make the mistake of thinking that a downward trend is necessarily accompanied by a low volume value, even if it is often the lack of volume that creates a descent of the price. Also in this case the two values are tied in way much tight one, therefore it becomes important, in the case it is wanted to invest aiming to the decrease, to verify that the level of the volumes is however low;

divergence between price and Volumes: this is the most interesting situation from the point of view of technical analysis, because it allows to make predictions on the trend over time of an asset. The divergence is used by the trader because it has the tendency to indicate the probable exhaustion of a trend. In particular, the concept at the base of this theory is given by the fact that without consistent volumes, it is unlikely that a trend has a long duration. Therefore, if the price is rising but the volumes are decreasing the bullish trend is destined to fall, while if the price is falling but the volumes are rising, the downtrend could be exhausted.

Combining the different tools of technical analysis with the analysis of volumes allows to have a wider overall view, giving the right indications on the operative strategies to put in place.

Chapter 7

Tools for Online Trading: Hardware and Software

What are the tools you need to trade online? Simply two, a personal computer (using a suitable software) and a connection to the Internet (ADSL at least 20 mega or Fiber Optic, definitely the fastest). There is no need to have the latest generation of instruments, with incredible computing power, or super-extra-fast lines, but the key word in this field is reliability.

Hardware

We have said that the key word, as far as personal computers are concerned, is reliability: therefore, especially for those who are less experienced in this field, it is better to rely on standard models, tested and normally fully compatible with different software and internal components. No problem instead for what concerns the type of personal computer: for online trading both notebooks (portable computers) and desktops (desktop computers) are fine: in this case it is a choice dictated by the opportunity and the space available.

However, it is important to remember one important fact: if you do online trading intensively, the best choice is to have a personal computer dedicated only to trading, to avoid having to install programs that can create problems for the system or cause it to crash. The technical characteristics of computers change at such a speed that it becomes very difficult to indicate a "perfect" configuration for online trading: it is always better to get advice from a trusted dealer, if you are not an expert, and remember the importance of having a monitor of excellent quality and the right size.

This is an important feature because in online trading you spend many hours staring at the monitor and choosing a good model avoids eye fatigue. Therefore, if possible, it is better to choose a model that is equipped with advanced technology (LCD at least, but much better to choose a LED model or higher) and has a high pixel density.

Another important note regarding the operating system of the computer: at the present time the Windows system is the most widely used in the financial sector. In particular, most of the client operating online trading platforms (which offer programs to be installed directly on the personal computer) are compatible with the different versions of Windows operating systems, while as far as compatibility with other systems is concerned (for example Linux) not all platforms offer a compatible client version.

Mobile devices

In recent years, the world of technology has been affected especially by the spread of mobile devices, such as tablets, smartphones and even wearable devices: many users have expressed the need to follow their investments also through these systems and many online brokers have adapted in order to meet these requests. The most widely used system has been the development of apps (applications), first born only with informative functions and then also becoming fully operational. In this sector there is a clear predominance of the iOS (Apple devices) and Android operating systems, while the influence of Windows and Microsoft in general is only marginal.

Although the power of mobile devices in many cases comes close to that of notebooks and desktops, there are still a number of inherent limitations (just think of the size) that do not make them the most suitable tools for a particularly active trader. However, they can be useful for monitoring and managing investments in all those situations where there is no immediate access to a "fixed" instrument.

The importance of an uninterruptible power supply

If you decide to do online trading intensively, you need to ensure that you can operate in every situation: and to do this, you need your work tool to be powered by electricity at all times. Therefore, the purchase of an uninterruptible power supply (UPS) is very useful.

These devices are able to provide power to the personal computer (thanks to the presence of an internal battery) even in case of a failure on the power grid: the price of these devices varies depending on the guaranteed power and the time of operation without power supply.

Operating platforms

When the personal computer has been equipped with an operating system, it is necessary to choose an online broker to be used for trading and then download and install the corresponding operating platform. This is a software that offers several possible functions to the trader:

- check stock exchange data (in real time in some cases), including a whole series of parameters (such as trading volumes and index trends) that are valuable for online trading;
- Choose which securities or instruments to invest in;
- Finalize orders and see that they are executed.

To be considered that as far as technical analysis and the choice of instruments to invest in are concerned, there are several specific softwares, independent from the operating platforms.

Platforms are divided into:

- basic platforms: they are used in the cloud (they do not need to install anything on the personal computer). Although they are normally slower and have simpler functions than client platforms, they are an interesting tool to start trading online. To use this type of platform, all you need to do is connect to a website, register and access the platform. It is a free type of platform;

- client platforms: these are the systems that offer the most comprehensive service for online trading. They are real software to be downloaded and installed on the personal computer. In some cases this is a paid service (monthly fee), which in many cases derives directly from programs developed for professional financial intermediaries and adapted for private users. Among the most advanced functions provided by this type of platform are the possibility of automated trading, virtual trading, development of indicators that are useful for analysis, such as charts. Some platforms, in addition to a large historical book of the performance of the various indices, also have a section dedicated to market news updated in real time.

Chapter 8

The role of the broker

When you decide to trade online, you need to rely on a broker: this figure is an intermediary who is the link between a trader and the markets on which the trader intends to operate. Since the broker's role is that of an intermediary, he has to execute the orders of his clients regarding the buying and selling of various assets on the markets. A trader gives an order and his broker executes it, buying or selling a particular financial instrument.

The figure of the broker is not born with the online trading: before the widespread diffusion of the net, for a trader it was necessary to go in person to the offices of the broker, during the opening hours, in order to carry out his investments. The advent of the internet has completely changed this system and favored the birth of online brokers: there is no longer the need for direct contact, but just a personal computer or other device to make trading, at any time and from any place.

The brokers have been able to fully exploit the potentialities offered by the net, going to create the platforms that offer to the clients not only the simple possibility to make trading, but also all those tools that can be useful to plan an investment strategy (like charts, news and historians).

Brokers can be:

banking companies: these often offer, along with online trading services, the possibility of using "classic" banking services;

non-banking companies: SIMs (securities investment companies).

Brokers can be divided into two main categories: the differences concern certain characteristics of the brokers themselves and above all the clientele towards whom the service is directed.

Broker Market Maker: the brokers who "make the market"

Market maker brokers are those who carry out their activity directly in contact with traders: to do this in the best possible way, they are able to guarantee the immediate execution of the orders forwarded by the traders themselves. The role of this type of broker is also to guarantee the liquidity necessary to finalize the orders: to do this, the broker uses its own internal market, which faithfully follows the trend of the "real" market.

This type of broker was born to operate with the public of the net: this means to work with a very high number of traders, that in their turn invest very small amounts.

Certain features distinguish market maker brokers from other brokers and make them an advantageous choice for traders:

- Costs: in most cases market maker brokers do not charge commissions on transactions executed on behalf of traders. Their profit results from the difference between the buying and selling price of a financial instrument (the so-called "spread"): this means that they make a profit whether the trader has profits or losses;

- guaranteed price: these brokers always complete orders at the price indicated at the time of the order;

- minimum investments: this type of broker allows you to operate even with minimum capital (often starting from 50 euros);

- user friendly platforms: the services of broker market makers are designed and realized to be fully accessible to the general public. In order to use these platforms it is sufficient to sign up and usually follow a simple tutorial introducing the functioning of the platform itself;

- Loss protection: this type of broker provides an automatic protection system for the benefit of traders, which is triggered when losses exceed the deposit. In this case the broker will close the trader's position in order to avoid further loss of money.

On the other hand, there are some features that may not be advantageous:

- spread system: the fact that the profit of these brokers is linked to both profits and losses of traders could create a kind of conflict of interest;

- limits to scalping: some traders set limits to scalping (buying and selling the same instrument several times during the same day);

- the risk of manipulation of the trade: the broker manages the orders of the traders on a sub-market controlled by him and this poses the risk of manipulation of the prices in the internal management, to the detriment of the trader.

ECN brokers: direct access brokers

The characteristics of ECN brokers are different: they do not operate on their own submarket, but directly transmit the trader's orders on the real market. Consequently, if the trader does not have enough liquidity for an order, it is cancelled, because the broker does not act as a guarantor of liquidity.

The audience with which these brokers operate is restricted, normally it is:

- professional traders (who invest high sums);
- investment funds;
- subjects that want to operate directly on the market.

ECN brokers have some interesting features, including:

- offer the possibility of scalping (provided the trader has sufficient liquidity available);
- the possibility of accessing the market directly, which is very important when large sums of money are invested.

The downsides to ECN brokers include:

- the fact that for each operation the broker requires a commission (to which the cost of the spread is added);
- the need to invest significant capital: ECN brokers normally require minimum investments of at least a few thousand euros;
- the fact that trading operations are more complex: the platforms of ECN brokers are not user friendly, but definitely reserved for experienced traders.

Chapter 9
Choosing the right broker

The choice of the online broker to rely on is an important and delicate step for a trader: very often, especially at the beginning of the trading activity, the temptation is to rely more on the instinct, limiting oneself to the collection of few and maybe superficial information (even only for "hearsay" or relying on the advertising of amazing services that the broker would seem to offer).

This is a system of choice that relies too much on impressions, often dictated by the haste to start trading, but losing sight of the many factors that must be involved in this assessment. Instead, it is necessary to ponder this choice with the right calm, taking all the necessary time and gathering the information you need to choose, considering both the offers of the different brokers and the needs you have in the field of trading.

Always keeping in mind an important fact: even choosing the "right" broker does not guarantee profits: online trading remains a speculative activity and if the broker complies with the contract stipulated with the trader and follows the rules imposed by the legislation, he cannot be blamed in any way for the trader's losses.

Choose only authorized brokers

It may seem a superfluous indication, but in the activity of online trading it is important to rely always and only on those brokers who are authorized to carry out the activity by the control subjects provided by the regulatory system (such as Consob and Banca d'Italia). This type of authorization only guarantees that the broker operates according to the standards of transparency and security imposed by law to protect traders.

It is not particularly important whether the broker is based in Italy or not, the important thing is that it has the necessary authorizations to operate on the Italian market: be careful, however, not to choose brokers who use a foreign language for their platform and customer service (unless you know it perfectly) because you risk misunderstandings and misinterpretations that can also generate important problems.

Factors to consider when choosing

Operational scope

If you have already decided in which field to operate with online trading (stocks, indices, currencies) it is important to choose an online broker that offers the possibility to operate in that market: in fact brokers normally do not operate in all markets, but often tend to specialize in a particular sector. For example, if you have decided to trade in binary options, it is better to choose a broker specialized in this sector.

The level of experience

In order to choose the right online broker it is necessary to base on the level of experience of the trader: for a beginner trader a market maker broker is surely indicated, as for a trader of medium level, while for an expert trader the choice can be that of an ECN broker (provided that he has an adequate financial availability).

The Platform

Although it is impossible to say that one online trading platform is superior to another (this is a choice where the subjective element has great weight), you should still ensure that you choose a platform that works without blockages and is user friendly, especially if you are not very experienced. A more experienced trader might prefer a more complex platform but with more functionality, in terms of choice of financial instruments and type of investment.

Deposit investment, investment lot and trade size

Each broker requires a minimum deposit to allow online trading, the amount of which can vary a lot: especially those who start trading tend to look for brokers who require low minimum deposits, for fear of being scammed by the broker. In reality, by choosing an authorized broker, you are protected from this kind of risk.

Directly related to the minimum deposit is the condition of the minimum lot, i.e. what minimum investment the broker requires: a high minimum lot also requires a high deposit, otherwise it becomes impossible to trade online effectively. If, on the other hand, one chooses a broker that requires a low minimum lot, no big investments are necessary.

Another related element to evaluate is the trade size, i.e. the number of contracts that each broker allows a single trader to open.

Leverage

Here is another aspect to consider carefully: if the broker provides high leverage, there is a greater chance of having good profits without necessarily investing large sums. Leverage is the instrument by which a trader is exposed to a sum of money that he does not have in his possession, money that is lent by the broker. Good leverage allows the trader to grow his position, resulting in increased profits. The downside is that as profits grow, so do any losses.

Trade-out

the trade-out is the level, fixed by the broker, at which a losing operation is closed: it serves to avoid the loss of large sums of money without the possibility of control.

Timing

Even if an online broker offers great conditions, all the benefits can be negated if the trader is not able to cash in on the profits made. A broker must always be absolutely punctual in transferring funds, both when they are deposited into an account and when they are withdrawn.

Costs and limitations

Another important aspect is the calculation of the costs that the broker imputes to the various operations: if they are too high, they risk "eating" the gain of the trading itself. Therefore, except in the case of an experienced trader who operates ECN brokers, a broker must always offer a free use of the platform, without providing commissions on operations. Its earnings should depend only on the spread, which is the index that also allows you to buy the various brokers.

The particular limitations to the operativity that some brokers can insert must be considered: in some cases they can prevent to carry out determined trading strategies, therefore better to know them in advance and to understand if they are compatible with the strategies that are intended to be adopted.

How to choose a broker: a practical system

A practical way to begin to untangle the various broker offerings is to ask yourself a series of questions:

- what do you look for in trading? In case you are approaching trading, the need is for a broker that offers a user friendly platform: you don't need special features, but rather a system that allows you to become familiar with tools and procedures.

- what does the trader need? A simple or complex platform, where a large number of instruments can be traded or specialized in a certain sector, which also integrates banking services.

- what does the broker offer? A wide choice of financial products, an efficient support service, the possibility to operate on a wide range of markets.

Answering these questions can allow you to understand which offer is the most suitable in the field of online brokers.

Leveraging demos

An interesting idea can be to take advantage of the possibility offered by different brokers to try a demo version of the platform, without investing any money, to understand if the broker is really suitable for the trader's needs, as well as to practice the functioning of the different tools. Obviously this is a time-consuming operation, especially if you test different platforms, but it allows you to avoid all those problems that you would have to face by choosing a service that is not suitable for your skills and needs.

Chapter 10

Operational Strategies

In concrete terms, trading online means buying and selling financial instruments (whether stocks, currencies, contracts) that are based on short and very short term movements, with the objective of obtaining a profit, which is based on price movements of a security in a short period of time. Obviously, each trader relies on his own personal strategy to achieve this result. A first distinction can be made between strategies that operate in the short term and those that operate in the long term.

A trader may choose to implement an active trading strategy that will allow him or her to make a profit. Obviously, there are several ways to implement a strategy, and each may be more or less suitable for a particular market sector. Whatever trading strategy you use, you cannot avoid the risk of losing your invested capital.

Popular strategies include:

Day Trading Strategy: it is a strategy, as you can already deduce from the name, that foresees the opening and closing of positions in the intraday (an interval of one day, 24 hours). It is a strategy to trade very quickly, but at the same time requires a study and analysis of the market behavior in the short term; when you decide to implement this strategy you can also decide to put into practice, within the same, a number of different tactics, such as trading following a certain trend or betting on a reversal of the trend itself.

Scalping Strategy: The so-called Scalping strategy operates on even shorter intervals than day trading. This strategy involves analyzing market volatility and selling and buying the same position at very short intervals, several times during the same day. This is a strategy that, in order to be effective and generate good profits, requires large trade volumes, which often can only be achieved by taking advantage of some important financial levers.

Buy and Hold strategy: this type of strategy is implemented by all those traders who operate on the long term and aim to get their profit based on long-term price movements, ignoring short-term fluctuations.

Why Use Strategies in Online Trading

In online trading the instrument you decide to trade is of relative importance, because there are two ways to get profits consistently: using a number of trading strategies and relying on the best capital management system. The importance of the strategies is central in this scheme, so it is necessary that they are techniques that have already been tested and that have been successful: relying on a trading strategy that has not been validated and tested with good results, very often risks leading to failure.

If one chooses to use a properly planned trading strategy, one can concentrate only on the data of the price fluctuations, neglecting all those news that, at market level, follow one another in a constant way and that often risk to cause confusion. In addition, following a strategy for a given period of time allows one to create a personal performance archive, which can also be useful for performance analysis and evaluation. And from this analysis it is possible to understand if the strategy applied is correct or if it needs any improvements to work better.

Online Trading Strategies: Social Trading and Copy Trading

Some brokers offer a further possibility, which is very interesting both for newcomers to trading and for those who do not want to put too much effort into studying investment strategies. Social trading allows you to study, thanks to a continuous flow of data and information, the strategies used by more experienced traders. The definition "social" comes from the sharing of this information, which allows even the less experienced to compare the different strategies and, eventually, choose to apply those of traders considered more experienced, trying to understand their modus operandi, without having to commit time and effort in complex processes of data analysis.

A further evolution is that of copy trading: it is a sort of derivation of social trading and it is a function that gives the possibility to "copy" the strategies of the most experienced traders and also to connect a part of one's portfolio directly with the trader followed. In this way it's possible to set an automatism for which the strategies followed by the trader are copied, in whole or in part: therefore, if the chosen trader obtains a profit, the same happens for whoever has "copied" him and the same happens in case of loss. Obviously it is always possible to intervene on the "copy" system, setting minimum and maximum limits and deciding how to distribute the risk within the trading portfolio.

Chapter 11

How to prepare for trading by choosing a security: book, charts, conditional orders, stop loss and order parameters

After examining the tools of online trading, technical analysis and having chosen which broker to refer to with their platforms, what procedure must be followed to "enter" the actual market? The tool to use is the platform, i.e. the system made available by the broker, which allows to use a whole series of functions (some provided by the broker, others directly related to the market). So there are three "variables" that each platform offers:

- the functions (basic or advanced): some platforms also allow the installation of additional functions thanks to third party programs or provided, with optional packages, directly by the broker;

- the possibilities and the limits to the operativity established by the broker (which can concern, for example, the possibility of operating only on certain markets or using leverage);

- the possibilities given by the market (for example, the limits to operations that may be present in certain hours).

The functions available on the platforms allow to choose a security (or other financial instrument) and the most suitable price level to send purchase orders ("enter" the market, as it is said in the stock exchange jargon) and to decide the most suitable price level, situation and timing to sell, either in whole or in part, the security purchased ("exit"): all this means to elaborate a strategy, which can be more or less complex.

Starting from the hypothesis of having decided to buy the shares of the company Xyx, which is listed on a market on which the platform allows to operate (for example the Italian market, MTA) when the price of the single share will be equal to 10 euros. The steps to follow will be:

Let's assume therefore that you are ready to buy shares of the company Abcdef (obviously this is a fictitious name) listed on the Italian market (MTA) at the price of 10 euros per share at the moment in which a certain market situation occurs, not better specified in order not to complicate the reasoning too much.

Now, the steps to take are as follows:

- locate the chosen security on the platform (normally using the search function in which to enter the name of the company or the initials of the security itself);
- check the situation regarding the security itself (i.e., whether there is any news that may affect the value of the security and in what time frame);
- check the price chart related to the security;

- check the book related to the price of the security;
- complete the order (by entering the data that are required by the platform, for example the purchase quantity);
- submit the order;
- check the correct execution of the order and the trend of the price of the security:

The first point is probably the simplest and the way in which it is completed depends on the specifics of the individual platform you are using. Also in this case the functions of the platform should be of help, allowing to identify a security showing securities, indices and markets organized according to homogeneous characteristics and selecting the appropriate "filters" that allow to narrow the field of choice. Some platforms foresee then of the systems of search particularly evolved, search that comes carried out selecting parameters also very particular: for example the Stocks that have a greater volume of exchange in a determined period of time or those characterized from one greater volatility.

Most of the available platforms also offer the possibility to visualize watchlists: these are lists of securities that are grouped together because they have homogeneous characteristics (normally, they are those securities that are part of the most famous stock exchange indexes, both Italian and international, such as the S&P 500 or the FTSE MIB). Many platforms allow not only to use pre-set lists, but also to create "personal" lists, based on parameters chosen by the user.

Check the book

The book has been for many years one of the most used tools by online traders: for this reason the different brokers have tried to offer the best possible service compared to the competition in this field. In order to understand how the book works, one must always keep in mind the overall functioning of the markets on which online trading takes place, which are based on two parallel flows, namely the purchase and sale of financial instruments.

We can imagine the book as a table: in the left part of the table are included the buy orders and in the right part the sell orders of the examined instrument (which can be a security, a contract, an index). In the left part of the table, which can be divided in three columns, there are the data related to the buy offer levels (also called "Bid" column) of the different traders: concretely, in this part of the table there is the price at which it is possible to sell a security in a given moment. In the right part of the table, always divided in three columns, there are the sale offers (also called "Ask" column): therefore the price at which it is possible to buy a security in a given moment.

The examination of the book shows that there are traders who offer certain securities at a certain price, while there are are other traders who are willing to pay a certain price for certain securities: all these data are based on the orders that traders, whether private or professional, submit to the market and are indicated by the price level and the time the order is received.

The first column on the left indicates the number of purchase proposals for a given price level, the second the quantity of securities included in these proposals and the third the price that the trader is willing to pay. In the right part of the table are indicated, in a symmetrical way, the number of selling proposals, the quantity of securities contained in the proposals and the price traders are willing to pay. The price of the left part is defined as money, the one of the right part as letter.

To the essential elements that a book must offer, i.e. number of proposals per price level, number of securities per price level and price level, many others can be added: to make some example, the elaboration of the trading volumes of the security and of the maximum and minimum price reached in a certain interval. Surely among the most important elements there is the one that gives the possibility to trade directly from the book, sending orders to the market.

Check graphs

The price of a security varies continuously and these variations can be represented in different ways: the book is one of them and the chart is the other "main" tool for data representation, which has become one of the iconic symbols of online trading. The charts that are used for technical analysis can be different, starting from the classic two-dimensional charts, with trend from left to right, with the flow of time marked on the x-axis and with the price positioned on the y-axis.

In the various charts (which can also be bar charts or Japanese candles charts) they can show a histogram at the bottom representing the traded volumes of the security: moreover the charts, when presented in real time with the market trend, update either with a frequency predefined by the platform or with a frequency determined by the user. The frequency can vary from tick by tick, which takes into account every minimum variation of the price, even if it occurs in a very short interval, to that of a time span that includes several years.

The most popular charting systems used by traders are:

- linear graphs: for which each period corresponds to a point and the various points in sequence form a line;

- bar chart: each period is indicated with a vertical bar with two horizontal lines: the highest point on the bar is the maximum of the security reached in a given period, the lowest point is the minimum of the security and the two horizontal lines represent opening and closing of the period. It is also possible to use different colors for the bar in case of positive or negative trend of a security;

- Japanese candlestick chart: seen in the chapter dedicated to Technical Analysis.

Linear charts are surely the easiest to read and the most used by traders at the beginning of their activity, while bar and Japanese candlestick charts are much richer in information and therefore more useful for an effective analysis.

Among the most popular functions in the various online trading platforms there is the one that allows to superimpose to the different charts the different tools used in technical analysis (like moving averages for example). In this way, also using the algorithms often proposed by the platforms, it becomes possible to evaluate the historical trend of a security, information that, if processed in the correct way, can be useful to predict the present and future trend of the security itself.

Among the functions provided by the most technically advanced platforms there is the chart trading, i.e. the possibility to trade directly from the charts: it is a tool very similar to the book trading, through which it becomes possible to send orders at the same time when the preferred trading price level is detected on the chart.

Conditional orders and stop loss system: order parameters

At a first impression, placing an order in an online trading platform may seem a simple operation: in reality it is not so, because often, to the basic order (which must include quantity of the security, price and indication of purchase or sale) you can add different functions, some of which are very important.

complex.

We can think of the case in which we decide to sell 100 shares of a company at a certain price: in fact, in addition to sending the trading proposal it is necessary to instruct the system how to behave in different situations that may occur. For example, no trader may be interested in the proposal and it is necessary to determine for how long it should be kept valid. Or there is a trader interested in buying only 50 shares and in this case it is necessary to decide whether to conclude the negotiation or not.

These are just two of the cases that can occur when trading online and the different markets provide the possibility to place different types of orders, although not all brokers allow you to place all the types of orders that are available. The various order types change according to parameters that can be modified, also it is possible, in some cases, to combine different order types.

The most commonly used parameters are:

- order execution phase: a day on the stock exchange is divided into various phases and in some of them only professional operators can operate. Among the most common phases there are the opening pre-auction, opening auction, continuous trading, closing auction and each phase has different rules for its functioning. So it is possible to send an order only for a certain phase: this order will be valid only in the time interval included in the phase;

- Security price: if you decide to trade a security at a specific price, a "limit order" must be entered. However, this implies that the order may not be executed or may not be completely executed. If instead you opt for the "at best" order you do not indicate a predetermined price, but you authorize the system to negotiate the security at the price that is present on the book at the moment of the order. Choosing this parameter it is much more probable that the order will be executed, but it is not said that the execution price is the one the trader thought;

- Time: it is possible to set different durations for the validity of the orders, starting from orders valid for a whole day (which are cancelled at the end of the day if not executed) to those that are cancelled at a specified date (unless they are executed before);

- quantity: within the quantity parameter there are different types of orders that can be sent: very common are EOC orders ("execute or cancel", whereby if the order is executed only for a part the rest is cancelled) and TON ("all or nothing", whereby partial executions of the order are not possible).

Conditional orders and stop loss

The tool of the conditional orders should be the most used by those who do online trading: these orders have the characteristic of "fulfilling" only when a series of conditions that the trader has imposed occur. This is a useful way to be sure that your trading strategy is always applied, even in those cases where you move "against" the trend of a security.

This type of orders are also known as "stop orders": they are those orders to exit from a position (therefore closing it) and that can be set to be "stop loss" or "take profit":

- Stop loss: these are orders that are set on an open position to close this position at a predefined level that is less advantageous than the current level of the security's price. With this type of orders the objective is to limit the possible losses related to the closing of a position and serve to shelter the trader in case of a sudden drop in the value of the asset;

- take profit: these are orders that are carried out when the price level of an asset reaches a predefined level. The objective of this type of orders is to make a profit from the growth of an asset, without exposing oneself to the risk of a subsequent trend reversal.

A further evolution of this type of order is the trailing stop order: it is an order set on an open position, with which the trader can set a stop loss point at a fixed margin from the market price. Consequently, if the price of the asset moves towards an increasing position, this movement will be followed by a change in the stop point, always maintaining the same distance between the stop loss point and the market price.

Chapter 12

Risk Management in Online Trading

When you decide to trade online you must also consider with the utmost attention the aspect related to risk management: you must understand what it is exactly and how to apply the right techniques in this area to avoid losses (even very large) of your capital.

Starting from the fact that the online trading is a financial activity of risk and that often the market trend "disappoints" what are the hopes of the trader, it is necessary to focus on a cardinal point: in case the forecasts (and therefore the investments made) are wrong, it is necessary to manage not to lose the capital completely. A use of risk management techniques allows to prevent part of the risks that one necessarily incurs when deciding to invest in the market.

What is risk management

When we talk about risk management, we mean the continuous process of identifying, analyzing, evaluating and managing exposures, losses, risk control and resources at the financial level, all with the aim of minimizing losses and the negative effects that result: therefore, in concrete terms, with risk management we seek to maximize profit and, at the same time, reduce the risk of losses.

But what are the risks in trading that can result in losses? The most common risks are:

- Financial risks;
- Operational risks;
- Risks associated with the political-environmental situation;
- Risks associated with the strategies implemented.

The objective of risk management techniques is to minimize all those factors, internal or external, that may prevent the trader from making a profit. Obviously we must always keep in mind that "accidental" losses are still unpredictable and often inevitable, but there are techniques that aim to make these "risk" events more predictable. Being able to do this means preventing or limiting the risk or, at least, estimating the losses that may result.

In fact, what is most often achieved with good risk management is to make unavoidable losses much more predictable, thereby securing the capital being invested (if not in full, then at least in part). To do this, it is important to monitor all the functions that fall under the risk management plan, so as to be sure that all are effective in reducing the cost of operational risk as a whole.

Theories of risk management: the fixed risk ratio

Several theories are applied in the area of risk management: one of the most popular is that of the fixed risk ratio.

This strategy works by purchasing a certain amount of units (of securities or other assets) relative to the capital held. This is a valid theory that can be applied for managing the risk of losses. To better understand this theory better to rely on a practical example.

Starting from the choice to buy one asset for every 5000 euros of capital owned: when your capital increases by another 500 euros, you automatically buy a new asset. This type of choice brings with it advantages and disadvantages. Among the former are:

- is a system that is based on a simple, linear calculation method;

- allows for a mechanical approach, which is especially useful to newbies to online trading because it allows you to not worry about sizing your position;

- Following this strategy, risk exposure increases only when there is an increase in overall capital: in this way, the level of risk remains constant over time.

Disadvantages of this strategy include:

- Following this strategy it is not possible to increase the exposure based on the exit probabilities. This means the same exposure for each type of trading probability;

- In the case of positions consisting of limited capital, the application of this strategy leads to the need for more time before being able to increase exposure.

Risk strategy as a percentage

At the base of this strategy is the amount of risk that each trader can consider tolerable

This strategy is based on the amount of risk that is tolerated for the trade. The percentage of risk tolerated can range from 0.1% up to 5% in most cases (although experienced traders tend to maintain a low level of risk). When setting a predefined risk percentage, make sure to keep the level of exposure the same.

To give a practical example, having a capital of 100,000 euros and choosing a risk tolerance of 0.5% for online trading, you choose to invest on an asset pair (currencies or indices) Y, where the value of a pip (i.e. the standard unit to measure the change of an exchange rate) is 5 euros. A stop loss is set at 25 pips.

In this case the tolerated risk on 100,000 euros will be 500 euros.

Tolerated risk for each asset will be 25 pips to the value of 5 euros, so 125 euros.

500/125= 4: means that 4 contracts can be traded at a time,

keeping the same level of risk. Advantages of this strategy:

- Applying this strategy you can always have a certain amount of risk, regardless of the stop loss value;

- it is a strategy that can be easily calculated;

- Through this strategy you can increase the number of positions gradually, always maintaining the predetermined level of risk, identified as a percentage of capital.

The major disadvantage of applying this risk management strategy is that it does not allow you to increase your risk exposure based on the probability of an outcome occurring.

The importance of risk management

Above all, traders entering the market have the tendency to consider only the profit they can get from operations, forgetting to evaluate both the size of their invested capital and their exposure: they just invest, often without even following a clear and well-defined strategy. But this is no longer online trading as much as it is real gambling.

To follow this line means not to think about the return of investments in the medium and long term, but to limit oneself to the search of the "scratch and win" billionaire: in reality this type of trading, which absolutely does not take into account the risk management, is the easiest system because the losses quickly exceed the profits, with the consequent loss of capital.

To understand the importance of proper risk management we can think of a casino, where many players manage to make million-dollar winnings: despite this the casino always continues to earn. This happens because in the management of the casino is applied a very good risk management, so that the losses resulting from the winnings of players are always lower, especially in the medium and long term, the total revenue, which comes from the losses of other players.

In online trading it is important to always be the casino and never the player: this is the only way to guarantee a profit from your investments.

How to apply risk management to online trading

Obviously, online trading is very different from gambling (if done correctly), but the risk management techniques are very similar. In particular, when trading online it is always necessary:

- analyze the context in which you operate: therefore, in addition to technical analysis, never forget the fundamental analysis (even if it may seem unnecessary in the short term), without forgetting to take into account all those unforeseen situations that may change for the worse the general situation. Attention then to "move" before market mover traders (i.e. those who move market trends) decide to upset the market itself;

- limit the risks: never invest in trading the sums destined to the satisfaction of the primary needs of oneself and one's family. This is a risk that should never be taken;

- each trade must have a clear and defined objective, so that the risk/reward ratio is always in favor of trading;

- the profit that can be made from an operation must be at least equal to the possible losses or, better still, greater. A good risk-return ratio is 1:2, i.e. looking for a profit that is at least double what you are likely to lose;

- never forget to use the stop loss tool: starting operations without using this parameter is the easiest way to expose yourself to too much risk and get in a short time to zero your investment;

- the investment must be proportional to the capital available: any potential loss must never exceed 5% of the capital;

- Always be patient and clear-headed is crucial in online trading: do not get carried away by emotions, but always follow the strategies planned in the right way.

Investing In Real Estate

BOOK 4

TABLE OF CONTENTS

INTRODUCTION

Many of us aren't going to be rich or millionaires from just working on our jobs. We have a little amount of time for active working. To achieve our financial independence, we have to develop alternative sources of passive income. Real estate investing can generate big profits and multiply your net worth.

Just like investing in the stock market, real estate investing can also be exhausting. However, there are just a few fundamentals that you need to master before you get started.

When you invest in real estate, you expect that the money you put to work today should grow to more money in the future. For many people, real estate is a great option to diversify their portfolio and generate some income at the time of retirement, or even beginning a new career.

Investing in real estate may appear as something only the rich can do. But the fact is that daily investors can always invest in real estate. You may not purchase a multi-million-dollar property, but you can invest in a starter house, clear the mortgage, and then rent it for some profit when you purchase the next house.

Real estate can be a bit complex than just buying mutual funds using 401(k). So, while daily investors can channel their money into real estate, you shouldn't do so until you have a plan that guides you on what you are doing. In this book, you will be guided on the steps you should take to invest in real estate. The first chapter will look at the basics of real estate, to give you a clue of what you should expect in the rest of the chapters.

CHAPTER 1

Introduction to real estate investment

R eal estate investment is considered by many as the easiest form of investment. One of the reasons is that there is a good exchange between the tenant and landlord. As long as the place of stay is good, and the landlord receives his or her due on time, life runs smoothly. But real estate investment is a bit complex than this.

If you make up your mind to invest in real estate, your goal is to invest your money and grow it so that you earn more. You have generated enough profit that will cover up any risks and other costs of owning a real estate property. This chapter will introduce to you the basics of real estate to help you gain a rough idea of how investors make income from their real estate enterprises.

In most cases, people start real estate investment to secure their future. Additionally, some set up real estate businesses as a passive income investment. In other words, real estate investment supplements their main source of income. Besides other investments, investors have dived into properties such as apartment units, houses, and other forms of real estate to expand their portfolios, earn more income, and plan for their retirement.

Some people look at the home they currently stay as an investment, which may appreciate after a few years if the housing prices rise. Others may invest in real estate by buying property to lease to a business to earn income via the rental payments that the individual provides. This is referred to as investing in "real property' and is one of the easiest methods to generate income through real estate.

Investing in real estate is far much better than the traditional investment system. In the traditional investment system, the property owner has the responsibility to process all the paperwork, search for a tenant, and perform any repairs. Owners of property are still accountable for all costs tied to the property.

Since the traditional system of real estate investment demands time, and money to pay for the property, it is better to invest in real estate using trusts, and other forms of investments that don't demand your time. When you invest through trusts, you don't need to maintain and manage properties. Instead, there are people employed to do this on your behalf.

So, why should you invest in real estate?

In recent years, people have joined real estate investment as a means for alternative income, and gaining profits that they may never have achieved through normal investments like bonds and stocks.

So, real estate investment is a far better investment that can provide a continuous stream of income over a specific time. Rent is a fixed income that you agree with the tenant, and you get paid every month.

Investment in real estate can still be a means to diversify an investment portfolio. Adding real estate investment into a portfolio of diversified assets, it can regulate the whole risk, and thus help investors to eliminate risks in their portfolios without affecting returns.

These features make real estate investment an efficient tool to diversify portfolios. However, just like all investments, there must be risks and uncertainties, real estate investment is not an exception; you have to be ready for some serious.

The 5 big reasons why real estate investment is awesome.

1. Income

This was going to come first because it's the main reason why everyone wants to take part in real estate investment. If you follow every step correctly, real estate can generate a huge stream of income that is enough to pay all your bills and save for your future.

If you own several multi-family buildings, each of the units occupied by tenants creates a stream of income. The tenants pay rent at the end of each month, and that income flows to the owner account.

This point is important because it defines the long-term.

Many people have a goal to save for retirement. Therefore, they try as much as they can to save enough money so that one day, they can replace the current income with their job, and stop working.

In other words, every time you buy a real estate that pays you a certain income you move a step close to your goal of income replacement.

You only need to get to a point where the income you earn from your properties is enough that you don't need to work anymore.

And then you can call it quits to your 9-5 job.

One of the main problems that people experience when they are planning for retirement is how to build a stream of income so that they stop working.

People work for years to create a retirement "nest-egg," and then they fail to identify the best way to turn the "nest- egg" into a running stream of income. But real estate is the answer to this problem.

2. Depreciation

Depreciation is an accounting technique that will allow you to reduce the value of an asset over its life.

For example, assume a farmer who buys a tractor to support his or her business. The reality is that the tractor is only going to last for several years until the farmer may have to buy another one. In this case, the IRS lets the farmer cut a certain percent of the cost of the tractor from their taxes every year as a business expense.

But the magic of real estate is that you also reduce the value of the property, but with time real estate rises in value as opposed to the tractor which becomes worthless.

As a result, you get a tax reduction to offset the income the property is generating for you, allowing you to save money over time. That is awesome.

3. Equity

Every time you pay for the mortgage, part of it is used to pay interest on the loan and another percent is used to pay down the principal value of the property. For every payment you make, you own more of the property.

If you own different rental properties, and all are occupied with tenants, the income you get from the rentals will pay your mortgage investment, and the remaining amount will be used for repair, maintenance, and other needs.

When you are done with the mortgage, you will own the whole rental property, and your tenants will have paid for most of the cost.

4. Appreciation

Besides the build-up in equity from paying down the mortgage, you will also earn from the rise in property value. After some years, the real estate prices increase in value. For example, between the 1960s and 2000s, there has never been a single year of decline in median home properties in the U.S.

Every part of the country is a bit different, but besides the high-appreciating places like popular cities, inflation also increases the prices of things over time including real estate.

5. Leverage

Leverage is a technique that you can pay for something without cashing out the entire cost. For the case of real estate, you can apply leverage by including mortgage to purchase a property and only pay a fraction of the total cost.

Though you only pay a small percentage of the buying price, you are accountable for All the benefits.

You will still earn all the income generated, all the equity created, all the appreciation of the property, and you make use of all the tax write-offs.

This is something that you can't achieve with other types of investments. There are few methods to purchase financial investments using leverage beyond the margin account, and there are other problems to worry about when you use it. But that is not going to be covered here.

The acquisition of leverage in the real estate market is what allows you to begin investing before you amass a fortune.

Different ways to invest in real estate

Now that you know the reason why you should invest in real estate; here's how you can get started. There are a lot of options available for you if you want to start in real estate investing.

1. Real estate investment trusts (REITS)

REITS own and run the real estate. They own large properties like office buildings, apartments, warehouses, and shopping malls. REITS are different from other real estate companies because they don't build properties to resell later, but their goal is to buy real estate properties to manage.

This means if you decide to invest in REIT, you will be eligible to earn income through payouts that trusts get from the properties they own. Investment in REITs can either be public or private.

For the public REITs, they are often exchanged on public platforms. For private REITs, the shares aren't posted on an exchange platform but are sold in an exclusive market. This is why they are very risky than public REITs. Being an investor, you have to fulfill certain requirements before you can start to invest as a private REIT.

Whether you invest in private or public REITs, both have risks that might impact the investment. Since private REITs aren't available in public, they have a higher risk than public REITs.

Risks of public REITS

Changes in rates of interest

When the rate of interest increases, REITs make less profit, and the reason is that their demand goes down. In this case, you will need to stick to your investment for some time.

Rental risk

REITs depend on rent they collect from real estate property they run. In this case, when a property owned by REIT remains unoccupied for a long period, the profit earned by REITs is affected. This translates to lower income paid to investors.

Risks in private REITs

Low liquidity

Private REITS aren't available in public. Therefore, it's hard to know the exact value, and it can't be easily traded. As an investor, you have to hold on to your investment for some time.

No transparency

Unlike public REITs that are subject to disclosure requirements, private REITs aren't. In fact, there is little information on how private REITs run. As a result, it is not easy to know how the REIT is performing.

Reduction in investment value

The payouts you earn and the value of the investment are affected by the property value invested by the RIET. In other words, if there are tenants who don't pay their rents or higher rates of vacancy may impact the number of payments.

Personal liability

You may be held accountable for clearing the requirements of private REIT if the REIT doesn't have funds to meet its costs. This is referred to as "capital call."

2. Real estate limited partnerships

These are also known as "LPS," and are popular for building and managing property already built.

LPs are under the supervision of a general partner. This individual uses the money collected from investors to buy land, and build properties. They can still sell it at a higher price than what they bought.

For investors, they can buy units in real estate LPS. A lot of these units are private and aren't traded on an exchange. Additionally, they are difficult to estimate the value or even resell it.

Common risks of investing in real estate LPs

No guarantee

Since the value of real estate changes with time, it's not a must that every project you invest in will generate profit.

Operational risks

Real estate LP depends fully on the ability of the management that support the partnership. For that reason, investors have a passive responsibility and are limited to the investment they have made. In other words, investors have no active role in the business partnership.

No diversification

Some real estate LPs develop single projects for a given period. Therefore, if the project is partially done, you might lose a specific percent of your investment.

Approvals of the government

Some real estate LPS don't have government permits to allow them to build on their land. Sometimes, they are denied permits, and this affects the investment value.

Risk of capital

Projects that go past the set budget may force you to invest more money to cover extra costs.

Mortgage investment entities

These are mortgage finances that tap money from investors to loan individuals who may fail to acquire a mortgage from traditional lenders such as credit unions.

Mortgage investment entities (MIEs) offer loans to borrowers using money collected from investors. These loans build the portfolio of a MIE and consist of residential mortgages like family houses, condominiums, townhouses, and commercial mortgages.

MIEs make money from the mortgage interest, mortgage renewals, financing fees, cancellation penalties, and other fees deducted from borrowers.

If you are an investor, you buy security produced by the MIE, essentially in the form of shares, restricted partnership units, or even trust units. These securities acquire value from the value of the underlying pool of mortgages secured by the real estate properties. You are allowed to get income from the revenue received by the MIE via its portfolio of mortgages.

Majority of the MIEs are private and don't have their securities listed on an exchange, making it hard to trade and value.

Risks of investing in MIEs

High-risk loans

MIEs usually offer mortgages that have a higher risk than mortgages generated by banks. In case a lot of borrowers fail to make their mortgage payments, the value your investment can drop, and the MIE may fail to offer you with any income.

Lack of liquidity

Most MIEs are private and not publicly traded, and that may make it hard to value and cannot be resold easily. You might have to stick to your investment for longer than you may have planned.

No guarantee

Certain MIEs claim to provide high annual yields and market investments 'secured by real property.' Secured doesn't imply that it's guaranteed, and though the real estate might directly support the mortgage, your investment isn't secured. Therefore, you don't have any rights to the property that secures the mortgage.

In case a borrower fails to make payments on a mortgage, this can damage the strength of the MIE to manage payments to investors and will affect the value of the investment. There are still many factors that can affect the success of and profits from a MIE. Past performance doesn't indicate the future returns of an investment.

High-risk loans

MIEs usually generate mortgages that have a higher risk than mortgages made by credit unions. If many borrowers don't pay their mortgage, the value of the investment drops and the MIE may fail to generate any income.

Drop in investment value

Borrowers can default on their mortgages or repay it sooner than expected, both of which can impact the value of your investment or even the amount of income that is paid out to you.

Low priority of rights

Borrowers can get second, or third MIE mortgages, which can be a bit risky. So, if a borrower doesn't pay for their mortgage, and the property is liquidated, the lender that released the first mortgage will be the first in the queue to receive the money back. The MIE that offered the second mortgage will only get the money back when the first mortgage is completely paid off.

Syndicated mortgages

These types of mortgages are offered by two or more investors that have invested directly in a single mortgage property.

As opposed to MIE investment, a syndicated mortgage investment only works for a single mortgage, instead of a portfolio mortgage. Some syndicated mortgages are used to support large-scale real estate development projects, for example, a high-rise condo building.

Risks of investing in a syndicated mortgage investment

There is no guarantee of high return

Though some syndicated mortgage investments may claim to provide 'guaranteed' high returns, these claims are false and not authorized by the law. All investments have a specific risk, and the higher the probability rate of return, the higher the risk of investment.

Secured doesn't imply it's guaranteed

Certain syndicated mortgages are said to be 'safe,' or 'fully secured.' Though it's true that your investment will be used to build a mortgage that is registered and secured with a building, if anything goes wrong with the project, and the value of the investment is restricted to the value of the land-you could rank behind other lenders and you may fail to receive any or all your money back. The reason is that the value of the land could only be sufficient to pay any prior ranking lenders.

A queue for repayment

If you are a syndicated mortgage investor, you will always come second in line to receive your payment. In this case, if the project fails to go through, you may not have any money left over to be paid.

Interest payment risks

A syndicated mortgage borrower may not have all the sources of income to facilitate the mortgage's interest payments. If you are an investor, you will be dependent on the borrower to get extra financing.

Lack of investor protection insurance

The government or investor protection fund doesn't ensure the syndicated mortgages. This means that there is no means for you to get your money back.

Early withdrawals

In case you want to withdraw your money before the end of the term, a new investor may be required to take over your position, and there is no guarantee that there shall be an additional for resale.

CHAPTER 2

Finding Investment Properties

There are various types of rental properties in the real estate market. Each has its own advantages and drawbacks, and some do well in certain conditions than others.

To choose the best type of property for your investment, there are a few factors that you need to consider, and most importantly, some investment strategies work well for specific types of properties than others.

When you decide to invest in real estate, you may encounter different investment properties. But how can you choose the best investment property type perfect for your needs?

There are a wide variety of factors that will impact your decision including the size of your budget, property location, and many more.

In this section, you will start by learning the different residential property types and what's special about them and then look at the different investment methods and the types of investment properties that will match every strategy.

Single-Family Homes

These homes have detached dwellings that host a small number of people. Single-family homes are the type of residential located outside the metropolitan city in the US, and they are often surrounded by a yard. In addition, they have their own drive-through and appear attractive to all types of tenants.

In the urban sides, single-family homes can be a bit expensive because they occupy a massive piece of land than other types of residential properties. However, because single-family homes are popular in suburban places, they are somehow cheap considering that they have a yard that surrounds them, and in most cases, they have a private swimming pool.

Townhouses

These are popular in larger cities. They feature a terraced house and contain a small footprint on several floors. Though they are small in size, townhouses have an extensive living space because they consist of multiple floors, which may rise to 6 or more floors in certain places.

Townhouses can be more expensive where single-family homes are rare. This is common in cities where a piece of land is more expensive than in the suburbs.

Condominiums

Also known as condos, they are the most common type of non-apartments in metropolitan and urban cities. Condominiums are divided into different units over a massive piece of land, and they are often surrounded by common places such as swimming pools and private parks shared by individuals of the condo complex.

In general, condos are cheaper than other types of residential properties, but they also have rules and regulations when it comes to maintenance, taxes, and insurance.

Luxury homes

Luxury homes are modern homes designed to be comfy. There are different descriptions of what a luxurious home should look, with some people defining it based on where it is situated, size and architectural design. Despite this, luxury homes share one thing in common: they are more expensive.

In fact, they are the most expensive types of residential properties. In most cases, luxury homes are located in upper-class locations and beautiful places such as Miami Beach.

Apartment

An apartment refers to a self-contained house unit that occupies a given space of a building. Apartment is flexible, lower upfront expenses and free maintenance. Apartments exist of different sizes; some are large while others are smaller.

Bungalow

You have probably heard of a bungalow, right? If not, these are low homes that feature an extended front porch without any upper floor or upper rooms defined in the roof. One unique thing with bungalow is that they make it easy for the elderly, and little children because they have a single floor.

Beds and breakfast

These are private homes designed for guests to spend a night. It consists of an inclusive breakfast along with other special amenities. Bed and breakfast are special and differ by city and region. They offer a much better value than a hotel because of better amenities such as Wi-Fi, parking, room, and bath.

Cabin

In the past, a cabin used to be a small home developed from logs. But today a cabin refers to a vacation home. It is a one-story home. Cabins are known for being warm, cozy and relaxing.

Chalet

Chalets resemble cabins except that they are built with heavier angled roofs and paneled sides. In addition, they have been linked with mountain locales.

Cottage

A cottage as the name suggests is a small home. Cottages are constructed using different types of materials such as wood, wattle, and stone. Cottages are popular in rural and semi-rural areas.

Mansion

Mansion are large and expensive houses.

Hostel

Hostels are pocket-friendly rental properties that are shared by travelers. 4-20 travelers can share a room at a time. Hostels are affordable and offer the chance to interact with different people from all walks of life.

Studio

A studio apartment is a tiny apartment. This apartment comprises of a living room, kitchen, and bedroom that is merged into a single room. Studio apartments are cheap and efficient. Because the studios have a minimum space, this type of accommodation is convenient for a single person.

Different investment strategies

There a few investment strategies that every investor in real estate would prefer. Each investment technique carries its own pros and cons when you evaluate it based on the risk level, profit, and the amount of time required for every technique to happen.

Here are the three popular strategies including the advantages and disadvantages.

Long-term rental

These are the most popular investment strategies common for entry-level investments and new investors. Long-term renting is a method of investment that depends on buying a real estate property for the main goal of renting it out for 6 or more months. The property owner and the landlord would sign a rental lease with the tenants renting the house, and the tenants would start to pay a monthly rent to the landlord which can be used to handle the property expenses, taxes, mortgage, and insurance.

Long-term rentals are best for townhouses and single-family homes. Typically, they feature the lowest risk of any investment strategy, and once the mortgage is cleared, they can begin to generate a large amount of rental income every month.

The disadvantage of long-term rentals is that it requires a lot of commitment and time before it begins to produce a substantial profit.

Short-term rental

This type of properties resembles traditional rentals. However, a short-term rental is offered for a short period, usually days, months, or weeks. This kind of rental properties has become more common in the past years because of the rise of services, websites, and companies such as HomeAway, Airbnb, and VRBO.

The short-term rentals usually take advantage of all types of real estate properties, but the luxurious houses can be more profitable because of the above-average rental rates that a landlord can charge his or her tenants.

The biggest drawback of these type of properties arises from the fact that different cities in the US have specific laws and regulations that limit this investment technique. Therefore, it's illegal to rent out properties for short periods or allow it for a limited period every year.

Fix-and-flip

Fix-and-flip properties are the types of real estate properties that are in a bad state and require substantial renovations and repair before they return to a condition good for stay. This investment technique can be a better option for a real estate investor wanting to earn a quick profit on their investment type. However, they also feature a high percentage of risk because of the high amount of charges that have to be invested in improving the property and the unexpected costs that may emerge in the whole investment.

Condos are a perfect option for a fix-and-flip method because of the tiny size condos and affordable costs of renovation. However, any residential property can be a perfect choice for a fix-and-flip, excluding luxury houses.

While certain types of properties may perform well for specific strategies of an investment than others, they are always great opportunities in the real estate market that can be perfect for your unique type of investment.

What type of property is the best for rental?

Choosing the wrong type of property is like marrying a wrong wife. It can be very stressful, difficult to end the marriage, and damaging to your whole life.

But how can you tell the best property to choose? Probably questions such as:

What should you purchase? What things should you avoid?

Should you go for four or two bedrooms? How about garages?

Is color important?

These are some of the most popular questions that you ask when you are about to purchase the correct deal and have the highest success as a landlord. Well, let's look at some things that you need to consider when you shop for a rental property.

Remember, everything being discussed here relies on the current trends in your location. In addition, this list isn't a bunch of rules that you need to adhere, but only tips that can serve you well.

Let's begin:

Bedrooms

Sometimes, it's hard to find long-term tenants in a 1-2-bedroom house. Single tenants prefer a one-bedroom, but when they hook up with a cute lady, they now need to move into a big bedroom such as two-bedroom. After some years, they get children and now need to move into a three-bedroom house. Therefore, three or four-bedroom house make the best rentals because they attract long-term tenants, reducing your vacancy expenses. Additionally, three- bedroom homes are the perfect type of property to sell, which can be the best when the time arrives.

If you are looking for a multifamily unit, two-bedroom houses are typically acceptable and popular. Single bedroom and studio are also prevalent but usually, attract many transient tenants.

Alternatively, more bedrooms aren't always a better choice. If you extend to five-bedroom homes or even more, you'll realize that the only tenants who want to rent them are families with many kinds. While kids are interesting and playful, many kids on property results in cases of broken windows, stained carpet and many more challenges. Therefore, you should try to keep a house to three-four bedrooms.

Age

If you purchase a very old property, be ready to pay a lot of costs in maintenance and fixing. Older houses also save less energy than new houses, which can increase utility bills. You may assume that it's not important because tenants are going to pay for their cooling and heating, but the truth is that tenants are aware of this. Therefore, if your property will cost an extra $100 to cool or hear, your tenants will do some simple math, and you may have a huge problem to maintain tenants in your property. This doesn't mean that you stop investing in older homes, but you just need to be aware that the older home, the more issues you will need to address.

Garage

When you decide to invest in single-family homes, it can be stressful to get a stable, long-term tenant to accept to live in a house that has no garage. Tenants usually accumulate a lot of things, and they need somewhere to keep them. Plus, places that experience a specific amount of rain, tenants enjoy the luxury of parking in a garage.

Homes that have garages stay occupied for longer than homes without garages.

Utilities

Certain properties, in particular, old houses, have utilities paid by the property owner, which is not a great option.

When you have little control over the house, adds a headache to your life. When tenants don't pay for the energy, they tend to misuse things. If they don't pay for water bills, they may never tell you about the leaking pipe in the bathroom costing you some hundred dollars every year.

For that reason, when you are searching for a single-family home, go for the ones which the tenant can pay utilities. When you look for multi-family homes, pick the ones where the tenant can pay heat and electricity, and if you can get properties that can be transformed into a "master metered" system that will permit tenants to pay for their water, you will have won for yourself some gold.

Lawn

Certain properties with gardens, large lawn, and other external amenities may never be attended with the same care as you would have done. Though every rule has some exceptions, it's good to look for properties with a small yard. That aside, recreational space is key in attracting a long-term tenant. So you should ensure that the tenant has a place where she can go to have some fun with the kids.

Parking

Stable tenants should have a place where they can park their vehicles. A driveway or even a garage is something that tenants like, so you should always look for properties with the above features. In general, two parking locations are far better than one, and so on.

Location

When looking for a property, keep a close eye on what's around. A tenant is just like you: they will want a place to eat out often, they will want to take a walk in the park, and they will want to buy some milk in the grocery store. They will also want to take their children to a great school, and commute less to their job.

They don't want to be hijacked, or stolen from. So you should purchase properties in places where tenants want to stay, and you will earn a stable rental income.

These are some of the features of property types that you should consider when purchasing a rental property. It is not a must to get each right to find a great rental property, but these aspects are crucial to pay attention to when looking for a property.

How to find investment properties?

Real estate investing is one of the best methods for building passive income. But for one to make a profitable income in real estate investments, it is important to know where and how you can find investment properties for sale that will produce a high return on investment. Being a real estate investor requires that you become resourceful, creative, and knowledgeable, so you need to know the different methods you can apply to find the best real estate properties.

There are different methods that investors can apply to find the best rental properties that are up for sale. By relying on a few resources, you provide yourself with the best chance to land the best investment.

Using networking to find a rental property

Not only is networking the best way to get profitable deals but also it offers a great opportunity to find rental properties that the general public may not know. Since not everyone knows about them, you have the chance to purchase these properties at a lower price. Important groups to the network include:

Personal investor network

This features a database of investors that you have been interacting with in the past few years, or you can start to keep from this time going forward. It can comprise of landlords whom you have interacted with or even old college friends who are now investors.

Investment clubs

Investment clubs are important contact because there is usually an email list where properties for sale are advertised or shared. If you haven't joined any clubs, it could be a great idea to join one. You can join a real estate investment club for a yearly membership fee between $100-$300.

Personal relationships

People in the real estate community aren't the only ones who can show you a great investment. Family, friends, and professional contacts can be great places to get possible investments. They could be experiencing a financial problem like a foreclosure, be aware of a person who knows of a property for sale. They may also have friends of their own who know important real estate investment opportunity. Your contractors can also be prospective sources to get leads because they can work for other investors that want to sell real estate.

Hire a real estate agent

Professionals exist to assist you with your investment. A real estate agent is a professional who knows exactly what to look out for in a property for sale. In addition, real estate agents access real estate resources that ordinary investors may not. Another way that a real estate agent can be helpful is connections. As you are aware, the real estate business involves networking with people. As a result, you cannot succeed without connections. An experienced real estate agent must have worked with different investors and other agents before. Therefore, he or she is supposed to assist you in finding rental properties for sale.

However, know that you may require to find a real estate agent who is experienced in matters to do with investment properties. Some agents may have worked with average homes, and that is a different story. It requires a professional to handle investment properties. Rental property investment deals require analysis of real estate property. From this analysis, you can determine the amount of return you can get on an investment property and select a profitable one.

Foreclosed properties

When thinking of how you can find rental investment properties, you should always remember to look at the local and national banks for foreclosed properties. Foreclosures, for example, make the best places for investment properties because they are sold at prices below the market value. Purchasing cheap rental properties lets real estate investors to attain a higher profit on every investment and can generate more money in real estate. And this is the purpose of every real estate investor.

Real estate open houses

You need to watch out for ads for real estate open houses in your local region and beyond. Real estate open houses are the best ways to find a property for sale instantly and to get an opportunity to ask any questions you may have before thinking of placing an offer on a property for sale.

Rental properties in print media

Print media is an effective method to find local listings. Some of these properties may not feature online, and so you will have little competition for them.

Newspapers

Newspapers are a handy source to get 'for sale by owner' properties plus Realtor listed on properties. You must ensure that you search for the main newspaper from your region, and other newspapers created for other specific cities.

Local marketing publications

You can get these smaller publications in most grocery stores. They are still a great place to land properties.

Auctions

Property auctions are another great place to find real estate deals. There are different types of auctions.

Online Auctions. You can look for investment on online auction websites like Auction.com.

Sherriff sale auctions: This type of auctions is done in the city hall of your county, courthouse, and hall of records. Foreclosures are first released to the general public at these sales. If no one buys the foreclosure at the auction, the foreclosing lender will own the property and list it as an REO using a local Realtor.

Private Auction Companies: For the private auction company, they are often contracted using lenders to sell a massive number of properties at a time. These auctions are advertised and conducted at a local hotel.

Finding rental properties using online tools and sources

Finding rental properties is something that many real estate investors have to Google search to get quick results that will provide answers to his or her predicament. No matter the kind of rental property that an investor shows interest in, they will at the one-point search for answers to this question.

However, this can be a bit difficult than it sounds. For example, if you type "rental properties around me," it may generate thousands of search results to select from, with a few rental websites and firms offering the same service, and each having a different level of quality. In fact, it's a big problem to find the best tool or website that will provide you with the best rental property.

But how can you select the best rental property online?

When searching for means to invest in real estate, the internet is one place where everyone turns to. As a result, the internet is the best place to turn to when looking for all types of rental properties. If you are looking for a house rental, then there is perhaps a rental website created to serve that specific function.

Some of the most popular searched words associated with real estate and finding investment rental properties include:

Condos for rent near me Foreclosures near me Townhomes near me

Typically, a few rental websites and companies have come up to solve these search phrases and offer homebuyers, and real estate investors with services and platforms that can be used to find any real estate property. Additionally, some rental companies and websites have focused entirely on specific types of real estate rental properties such as townhomes.

Despite this, real estate websites have increased in number in the last few years, and the reason is that many people are finding it hard to get real estate properties. As a result, the easiest channel to find rental properties is to look at online websites.

Types of house rental websites

While the main function of real estate websites is to help real estate investors and homebuyers to find rental properties, the tools, and services used by every website is different. Some rental websites offer more services than others.

Airbnb: This website is good for anyone looking for houses for rent for a short period. The invention of Airbnb resulted in an increase in the number of rental houses by personal homeowners. The idea behind Airbnb is to allow homeowners to become a landlord as long as they have an extra room or space that they think they can transform it into a rental house. The good side of this idea is that the homeowner earns a great profit from renting his or her house.

Nowadays, the hustle of finding a rental house is much easier than before because of the increase in the number of house rentals, and the development of rental websites that hook up investors.

There has also been the rise of rental property management companies that make work easier for real estate investors. The purpose of these companies is to manage the rental property on behalf of the investor, or homeowner. In this case, homeowners with rental far away from where they stay have no problem because everything is being taken care of.

For example, townhomes for rent have become popular places for real estate investors interested in rental properties. While these homes haven't been popular long-time ago, nowadays they have become a hot cake because of their remoteness and increased demand by travelers.

Other websites have entirely concentrated on renting out buildings and creating apartment finder tools to allow real estate investors to locate nearby apartments.

Using Mashvisor to find rental properties

Mashvisor was created to meet the needs of people, and to offer numerous services that can assist investors in finding houses for rentals. The site focuses on both traditional and Airbnb rental properties. It generates a long list of townhomes for rent, condos for rent, and other types of homes for rent. Whether you are looking for townhomes for rent near you or condos for rent around you, this site generates a detailed search result plus a map that will allow you to know the exact location.

CHAPTER 3

Flipping houses

The purpose of this chapter is to teach you more than a few steps you need to know to stay ahead of other house flippers. House flipping is a lucrative business, but you need to pay attention to detail to become successful.

Characteristics of a successful house flipper

Before you start to learn the steps, you need to follow to flip houses successfully, it is important to learn the traits of great house flippers. You can consider these as secrets of house flipping.

As long as you are committed, and dedicated, you will learn how to flip houses and generate profit. But as said before, you cannot purchase property without understanding the characteristics of successful house flippers. These are traits and skills that you must practice and apply if you want to make any profit and enjoy flipping houses.

Patience

Deals in house flipping run quickly when they start, but it takes time to land a deal that will earn a good profit. As a new house flipper, patience is critical in your daily operations because you will lose some money at the start, and slowly learn from your mistakes. The goal is to be patient and learn from every mistake you make, and then be ready to make some losses before you can get started.

Determination

A house flipper should be ready to learn something new for every house flip they make and then expand their network. You will also need to make all efforts to stay ahead of the competition all the time. You must show passion for house flipping to become successful because it will demand a great deal of your time to boost your business. Even when you succeed, you will still need to establish that intense edge to remain successful and expand your business.

Charismatic

If you didn't know, house flippers spend time in negotiation to land the best deal. As such, you must have a specific level of charisma to help you negotiate with lenders, buyers, contractors, and sellers. The main secret to developing the charisma is to become confident. Confidence arises from success. In other words, if you choose to master your trade and become the best flipper, then your confidence will start to show up when you negotiate deals.

Persistence

As a house flipper, there will be challenges that you will experience with your new project. Whenever these setbacks hit you, take a deep breath, look for a solution to the problem, and keep moving forward. As a new house flipper, you must know that you will encounter more than one challenge, and that should not make you give up on real estate business. To become successful in rental property investment, you must teach yourself to be persistent and fulfill your goals.

Let's now look at the Financial side of house flipping

One of the best things about this chapter is that you will learn everything that you need to know about house flipping. So at the end of the chapter, you will be ready to get started with house flipping. Keep in mind flipping houses isn't a get rich quick scheme, and it can make you lose all your capital if you aren't careful. It takes confidence and courage to launch a business in house flipping. Additionally, it demands great contacts for sources of funding and contractors.

Just like any other investment business, house flipping can eat all your money and leave you with nothing. This means if you get started with a poor plan, you may lose much more than what you input. If you select a house in a bad location and you fail to sell it immediately, then you could start to count losses right away. That is the reason why this chapter will take time to touch on every angle of house flipping that you must know before you can begin to flip your first house. This is done to avoid you making any losses while flipping houses.

One of the main reasons why a lot of people invest in real estate is because it can be a real gem once you get it right. Some house flippers boast of earning between $10, 000 -$100, 000 in profit on specific individual deals, and there are plenty of success stories of house flippers online. That is why it is advised that you look for a mentor who can present you with an actual account of their life story in house flipping including their failures. With house flipping, the odds for making a profit are huge, but you need to be always on alert to avoid making any losses.

House flipping rules that you must adhere to

In the whole of this chapter, we shall present you with a lot of rules that you must learn to assist you to attain success in flipping houses. When you stick to the rules of house flipping, you will realize that it's easier to get successful deals and buyers who will assist you in making a huge profit.

1. The more you spend, the more you should generate

If you decide to pump $40, 000 to renovate a home that will earn you $20, 000 profit, then this is not a great deal that you should involve yourself. Large renovation projects are done to generate big profits, and this is a rule that you must not forget whenever you want to purchase a distressed property.

2. Don't take on more than you can handle

For new investors, the first successful flip can create more expectations than expected. As a result, the investor ends up taking up a lot of projects, or even participate in projects that are beyond their potential. As said before, this is not a get-rich pyramid scheme. Instead, it is an investment where you develop on your experience by working on projects that you can handle and maintain your workload to an amount that you can successfully track all the time.

3. Don't leave anything to chance

You will go through a lot of information associated with planning your flip so that you don't get any surprise but only make a profit. The advantage of planning every aspect of your flip cannot be underrated. Once you gain some bit of experience, you will discover that the plans you set up for your flip will turn out to be the best path to success.

4. Always look for good advice

After spending a few years flipping houses, you will become confident while working on certain areas of your projects. But still, the most successful house flippers usually look for reliable advice from professionals to help them boost their knowledge base. Successful flippers don't think that they have all the answers because arrogance breeds losses.

5. Trust yourself

If you adhere to every step-by-step advice provided in this chapter and make it a habit to check and re-check your information, then you will acquire the confidence to trust every decision you make. You might start by making guesses, but the experience will help you to trust your instincts over time.

Knowing the fear you will feel

There's so much to say about the power of positive thinking when you flip homes. Real estate investing isn't a business for those with a weak heart, you must be committed and confident of seeing projects until the end. If you want to involve yourself in house flipping, then you must know how to manage the mental setbacks that will always pop-up in the process. The first emotion you will need to deal with is fear, and it can take some time before you get in the right mental state to conquer the feat that comes with house flipping.

Fear itself

The single important reason why people ditch their dreams of house flipping is fear. And fear is the main factor that prevents people from fulfilling their potential. The first thing that happens to your subconscious mind when you take a look at house flipping is to challenge your motivations and worry related to the possible outcomes. Fear is that type of hesitation that will cause you to stop and begin to ask yourself questions. That is the reason why being educated about house flipping is critical.

You are probably reading this because you have made up your mind on a decision that is causing fear inside your heart, or you want to discover more about house flipping and assess whether the fear you have is true. It is normal to challenge yourself or doubt yourself when you want to flip houses, but it is crucial that you eliminate that fear if you want to become successful. So, let's start by finding out the different types of fear that may arise when you get started with house flipping.

Common Fears

Simply because something is known all over doesn't mean it is understood. You may identify all the types of fears involved in house flipping, but we shall assist you to overcome those fears and get on the track of making money.

The house fails to sell

Each fear related with house flipping can be overcome with effective planning. Many new house flippers fear that a house may fail to sell, so they disregard the investment. In the whole of this chapter, you will learn exactly how to recognize homes that can sell quickly.

This chapter will also teach you on steps to take to sell your property fast at a reduced profit and means to make money with your property while still on the market. Even if your house doesn't sell immediately, you will still have numerous options to make a profit.

Running low of cash

Nothing is so frustrating than a house flipper running low of cash before completing the first project. The right way you fund a house flipping project is to plan your remodeling money, purchase money, and to hold costs in the bank. You should not over-plan your house flip when you collect all your funds together.

When you gather your remodeling budget, make sure that you set aside around 20 percent to deal with unforeseen circumstances. If you aren't sure about your abilities to define the needs to be done for a successful house remodeling, then it's better to look for a professional. Once you hire a professional to assist you in planning your remodeling project, then you will save some money in the end.

Holding costs refer to monthly bills that you pay as the property owner, such as utilities, mortgage payments, and maintenance. When you organize your house flip, ensure that you also set aside three months of holding costs in your budget. So if the house doesn't sell after three months, then you should sell it to a wholesaler or rent it out for a fixed amount. You have choices when it comes to money, so you should not be worried about running out.

Lose cash on the deal

So far you have learned something on how to eliminate the fear of losing money on a flip, but there are some tips on how you can eliminate that fear for good.

Add 20 percent to the numbers you develop for your flip budget steps (purchase, remodeling, and holding). If you are working on a budget with the purchase price, then you will have some extra to channel to the remodeling project and holding expenses.

Keep in mind that landing some funding from a lender and outlining the property via a real estate agent may also have costs related to them. Don't forget to put the costs in your budget.

If you are unsure how correctly estimate the value of a home, then register for a real estate course. The investment will assist you in estimating the values of property and avoiding overpaying.

If you decide to purchase properties using foreclosure auctions, keep in mind that you will often not be allowed to look at the interior of the property before you can place a bid. Foreclosures can be a gold mine if you really know whatever you are doing, but you might want to look at various auctions that happen before you place bid yourself.

There is nothing like too much planning for a house flip. If you plan to eliminate the fear of losing money, then you should ensure that you learn everything you can relate to housing flipping before you begin and continue to learn every day. Always make the necessary plans on every project, and make arrangements as possible. There are no secrets to success in house flipping, so don't look for the easiest ways.

The fear of setbacks to remodeling

Some people see a house in a remodeling stage and decide to destroy it. Others see a construction site and think like they have to steal everything that is not nailed down.

Your worries in remodeling can also stretch to other activities that you cannot regulate. If you find a stretch of bad weather, then you may need to close it down. If a person forgets to file for the permission rights, then the city or town you are in will close down. You need not fear such unknown contingencies since you will always be ready for them.

Insurance: You need to make your house flipping business professional by integrating or at least completing a business certificate, and next insure your operations. You can speak to a commercial insurance sales professional about insurance to safeguard against theft, lost revenue, bad weather, and anything that you think of. Don't start a house flipping business without the correct insurance in place.

Great communication: If your remodeling worksite supervisor is permitted to stop work because of insufficient permission, then it is important for the supervisor to know how to strike a hold immediately so that the problem is solved. Effective communication between contractors, real estate agents, and investors can solve most flipping challenges.

Emergency funding: Suppose you want to stop a task just because you underestimated remodeling funding? If you own the credit lines, and other funding plans in place, then this should never be a big issue.

Fear should never prevent you from flipping houses because you can clear all fears using great research and detailed planning. When you decide to flip houses, your next step should be to combine the resources to start. The entrepreneur who expects success should never allow fear to get in the way to attaining a profit.

In the next part, you will learn more about how to handle all of your fears related to house flipping. You will go through comprehensive info to teach you how to change from being a hesitant investor to a brave entrepreneur.

Overcoming the fear of flipping

Once you know the fears associated with house flipping and the way those fears build, the next thing is to overcome those fears and start working. As said before, you must have a detailed knowledge of house flipping before you can eliminate your hesitations and begin investing. Once you get started, the experience that you acquire will assist you in setting aside all fears and becoming aggressive and successful flipper.

Always develop a plan

It is said that having a plan in place will assist you in handling your fears, but what does that imply? Combining a plan for house flipping will work as a guide and assist you to avoid making costly mistakes. When you are a newbie to house flipping, it is hard to recall everything you need to ensure that a flip is successful. Your plan can work like a checklist that ensures you remain on track. The parts of a great house flipping plan comprise:

Selling prices- If you want to take part in neighborhoods that tend to sell properties at a profit, then you will require different online resources to identify the types of properties that appreciate in value in specific neighborhoods.

Selling out great Properties-A great neighborhood is but just half of the equation when it comes to generating profit while flipping. You must take time to comprehensively scan out every property in a neighborhood, and only handle properties that have a lot of room for making a profit. Purchasing a property that isn't distressed and selling at a close to retail will not allow you to generate profit. Keep in mind that simply because you remodel a property doesn't imply it will sell for the profit you want.

Neighborhood dynamics- Select neighborhoods with properties that sell fast. If you pick on a neighborhood that has a history of properties that stay on the market for over six months, then you will find it difficult to generate profit in that field.

Be great with numbers

House flipping requires that you are good working with numbers. You must know how to determine remodeling costs, know how profit is generated, and recognize when a deal is realistic. If you aren't well of with math, then you must set aside time to attend classes to boost your math skills. Experience working in a crunching real estate number will finally make you an expert in generating accurate computations, and you must always be open to new methods for applying figures you generate.

Every house flipping transaction has a pattern, and that pattern is:

Identify the amount of profit you want to generate before you participate in any property deals. Be alert in combining comprehensive figures that will make up for each aspect of the flip.

Maintain reliable notes on each mathematics feature involved in transactions.

Don't fear to consult with a professional if your numbers don't work out, or you aren't sure what you can do with the numbers.

Don't flip on your own

Many flippers avoid involving financial partners because they don't want to share any profit. That is a great entrepreneurial attitude, but it doesn't imply that you need to run your flipping business on your own. In the business sector, the most successful people know that they don't know everything and they ask for help from other people.

Real estate investors Association-There is an REIA group around you, and you must join it and stay as active as possible. Every member in an REIA takes part in meetings for the same reasons; to network with other investors and extend their opportunities. Certain REIA members are always happy to describe parts of the process you may not know, while others prefer to exchange information for the opportunity. If you would like to flip a house successfully, then you must be an active member of your local REIA.

Get a mentor- When you participate in REIA meetings or any other professional networking task, you will begin to speak to people who have attained a certain level of success that you would like to attain. When these people are ready to guide you, and show you the correct path to take, they become your mentors. When it comes to house flipping, nothing is more important than being able to make a phone call and get advice from a professional expert.

Online mentors- These refer to house flipping experts who reach to a large online audience, and they can assist you to boost your profitability. The challenge with online mentors is that many people want to scam entrepreneurs instead of giving them good advice. If you choose to acquire information from an online mentor, be on the lookout for people who ask huge amounts of cash for industry advice.

Try a partner- If you are getting started with house flipping, then it may be a good thing to try a joint project with an expert flipper for your first few projects. You may learn a great deal about the details required in house flipping when you become part of a partnership.

Give yourself a learning curve

Fear can always lead to frustration if you don't allow yourself to learn as you move along. Take every flipping project slowly, and realize that you will make mistakes in the first few projects. The secret is to learn from those mistakes and not to get angry at yourself for committing them. If you use your mistakes to improve your knowledge, then you will become a better flipper as time goes by.

What you only need to fear is?

When you are starting a new business that you aren't familiar with, fear is inevitable. The two steps that you need to deal with fear are recognizing that which scares you and then building a detailed plan to overcome the worries. For house flipping, the greatest fear that engulfs many new house flippers is the fear to lose all their money.

One thing that results in early anxiety on the side of the house flipper is the feeling that they are in over their heads. However, with the correct mentors and a strong partner to assist you in starting, you can learn as you proceed without leading to your business collapsing. The next thing to recall is that you will fail more than once when you get started. If you are aware that failure is coming, then you must use it to your advantage rather than fearing it. People who have made it in life learn from their mistakes, and apply confidence to get ready to conquer fear.

Building your investment criteria

The concept of planning for each house flip cannot be underrated as planning is the most step of any successful business. When looking for the correct properties, you must have an outline that you need to follow that will assist you in choosing the best investments. Although it is true that you are expecting, until the time you begin remodeling, you can highly boost your opportunities of generating profit by rapidly using the experience to improve your investment procedure.

The important elements of a great flip

In this section, you will benefit a lot by learning the important elements that you must consider to decide on whether or not to pursue an investment opportunity. Before you start to process any real numbers or involve contractors to develop estimates, you must identify whether the type of property you want has all the features of a great flip.

The correct location- The location of the property will define its value and the speed at which it will sell. If you want to get properties located in the neighborhoods where homes sell quickly, and home values appreciate fast. Do some research on the type of neighborhoods said to be the best to invest in and eliminate neighborhoods that pose challenges to your business.

A great foundation- As a house flipper, you must be ready to replace some drywall and perform roof repairs. However, you need a house that is structurally well and sits on a great foundation. Mold, damage to wooden house frame, and cracked foundation walls are red flags that you want to clear out.

A better school district-A house located in a school district with a characteristic for providing safe and effective schools will sell much faster.

The potential of a value- When house flipper spots a problem in an old home, they see the opportunity to make money. Homes lose value because of many things that are easy to correct. When you look at properties to flip, aim to pay the least possible for a house that can generate a strong profit.

Pay attention to market Trends-Market trends in rental business differ from one neighborhood to the next. You may come across a great neighborhood, but the recent houses for sale have stayed for months. Examine trends for every market and only choose to invest in neighborhoods that reflect an upward trend in home pricing.

Analyze your profit

The profit you generate will not always be the profit you want, but you must define a profit as part of your plan to house flipping. There are two methods to determine your possible profit:

As a set amount

As a function of remodeling costs

Many flippers determine profit based on a function of remodeling costs because it is an easier alternative to perform things. Let's imagine that you bought a foreclosed property for about $45,000. The retail value of the same property is $125,

000 and you think it will require around $35,000 to repair it. You estimate that it will require about three months to sell, so you factor in an extra $1,250 for different holding costs and transaction fees.

Your total investment would be around $83,750, and you approximate that it will sell for $120,000. This generates a possible profit of $36, 250, which may be a little more or less based on how quickly the property sells. Keep in mind that your remodeling costs may include a pad of 20 percent to take care of any unforeseen costs.

Now, suppose in this case, you choose to make $38,000 in return? When you decide to make a lump sum profit number, you must regulate all the numbers around it to ensure that it works. If it is hard to change the selling price, then you need to return to the remodeling plan and attempt to reduce the costs. Be keen when you choose to reduce the remodeling costs because those reductions will prevent you from selling the property fast enough to generate profit.

Another method to make a large profit is to buy the property as a distressed property and sell it to a wholesaler at a constant price. The wholesaler will want to sell the property to another flipper, so you may require to lower your profit expectations. However, when you want to make a quick profit on flipping a house, then using a wholesaler is the best path to take.

For you to attain your massive profit, you may need to consider getting a tenant while the house is still for sale. While this may be a bit hard to get a tenant who wants to sign a three-month lease, you can think about renting the property for a year and let the value of the property appreciate to attain a huge profit. Your tenant will handle your holding costs, and you may increase your profit by letting the property appreciate.

Holding expenses and fees

Holding costs refer to the expenses you pay at the end of the month to keep and maintain the property you sell. It is impossible to show a house unless it has the power turned on, and someone has to maintain the landscaping to keep the appeal. Monthly holding costs comprise:

Repair costs- When something happens to the property, such as vandalism or break-in, then you may need to assume the financial responsibility for performing the repairs. This is the point where another holding cost, homeowners' insurance, can become handy.

Maintenance Costs-Regardless of whether you decide to perform the maintenance yourself or hire someone, there shall be costs involved.

Utilities.

Homeowner's association Fees-You may have to think twice about attempting to flip a house in a gated community or any place that has association fees.

Mortgage payments-If you financed your property buying, then you will require a monthly payment to make sure that the property remains in your name. You may also need to pay monthly payments on any loans you take to perform the remodeling, and you will need to pay the related loan fees each month.

Many new flippers don't consider the long list of fees that occurs with flipping a house. Those fees comprise of:

Property Taxes-You will be accountable for paying the prorated property taxes when you sell the property.

Closing Costs-You may decide to shift your closing costs into your financing when you purchase the property, or you may pay them up front. These comprise of property surveys, insurance costs, legal costs, and title search costs.

Liens- In case there are liens on the property that the owner doesn't want to pay, then you may have to pay for them before the purchase can pass.

Code violations-In the remodeling process, you may compile a few code violations that must be paid before you can sell the property.

As you get ready to invest in house flipping, you must have a blueprint to notify you of the massive financial duties that are involved in house flipping. A written guide can act as a template to build a comprehensive budget, and your best method to avoid losing any money on a flip. Profit isn't guaranteed, but people who decide to plan these things out are meant to be successful.

Finding homes to flip

If you are a savvy real estate investor, finding great properties to flip is important as the flip itself. When looking for a great property to flip, your main goal is to find a distressed property or distressed owners. You will learn more about a distressed property, or owner, but the idea is that you want don't want to purchase properties that require a retail price and should perhaps get it.

House flipping is a business that needs a person to stay patient because you will have to consider at least three, or four options for each decision you make. You need to speak to different lenders, attorneys, or contractors before you choose on who to hire, and you need to do your due diligence when looking for properties. Although you may need to look for more than one house to flip at a time, you need to always factor at least three or four properties to offer yourself different options to select from.

What should you look for?

Before you can look for properties to flip, you must have a great idea as to what you are targeting. A distressed property refers to one that requires repair before it is sold for retail value. Many distress properties are abandoned for some time, which makes the negotiation of a purchase a bit easier. A distressed owner is one that is about to enter into foreclosure, or has experienced life changes that demand to sell their home a necessity.

Below is a list of various conditions that result in a distressed house and owners. Most of the information that you need to find these kinds of properties is available online.

Houses hit with the building code or zoning law violations.

Owners that have been forced to leave town and are desperate to sell their houses quickly. Homes listed as being in pre-foreclosure because of various missed consecutive payments.

Couples who have filed for marriage divorce and may be interested in selling their house at a discount. Get in touch with families of the recently deceased to assist them in selling their loved one's home fast. People convicted of a crime, or lost a major civil lawsuit, and cannot afford their homes at all.

Members of the military who are about to be deployed and might want to sell their home before they leave. Going to attend foreclosure auctions and placing bids.

Replying to classified ads for people who are selling distressed homes, and putting your classified ad in a local newspaper ready to purchase distressed homes.

Take advantage of online resources to get sellers of distressed properties and potential buyers if you want to sell a home without remodeling.

Go driving and look out for distressed properties in a specific area. The contact details of the owner should be in a file at a city hall in case the home is abandoned.

Learning more about foreclosure auctions

Before you can begin to place bids at foreclosure auctions, it is good to attend some and look at the way the process takes place. At an auction, you are not always given any additional time to take a look at how the property appears, and you won't be allowed to get inside. Therefore, if you know the address of the auction early, then you can attempt to take a glance of the property in advance, but still, you won't be permitted to get inside.

It is crucial that you are aware of the procedure of an auction before you decide to participate, or else your bid may get you in a huge hole that is hard to come out. Some auctions may need you to pay cash at the end, while others will allow you to have funding organized that would feature short term payments. Either way, you should be ready to pay for the foreclosed property the day you purchase it, and you may be requested to pay back taxes and any liens that are on the property too.

Innovative methods to find properties

Sometimes, it requires a person to go beyond the normal to get properties to flip. Part of the joy of flipping a house is building new methods to identify properties and see the same properties generate profits.

Search through a Multiple Listing Service (MLS) expired listings to get properties that are still on the market. In some instances, the owners may be ready to sell the property at a discount just to eliminate it.

Many banks have a Real Estate Owned (REO) department that produces lists of properties that emerge for foreclosure. Get in touch with banks and begin to request for their REO foreclosure lists.

Search for current MLS listings for properties that feature a large number of Days on Market (DOM) time. You may need to research your market to learn the way DOM time is too much, but the best rule of thumb is to get in touch with owners that have properties featured on the list for over a year.

When you investigate the MLS listings in your place, ensure that you get in touch with owners with listings that passed through different price changes.

Other possible property owners that you may work with are people who have recently closed down their business, people who have retired recently, and would like to sell their home to purchase a smaller one and any other situation where a property may be distressed.

Getting in touch with owners

Flipping homes is a mathematical game, and that means that you need to try and reach out to most distressed property owners as possible. One way to achieve this is by purchasing a mailing list depending on the criteria outlined, and then send out postcards to every owner who offers you their service.

Another great way to contact many distressed owners of distressed properties is to build a working association with many real estate agents as possible. You can provide agents with a finder's fee once a property is flipped; this implies that you would only pay as an agent for a property that is sold at a profit. Real estate agents can also be invaluable resources for getting buyers once a remodeling project is complete.

If you want to succeed in house flipping, then you must know the type of properties that will make the best inventory. Unless you have sufficient financial resources, it is better to keep your flipping projects to one or two at a time. Once you get going, you will find it difficult to turn deals down. But with time, you will build the experience and professional network that you require to turn every type of distressed property into a lucrative deal.

Finding and rehabbing a home

It requires time before an investor can find and purchase properties that make the best flipping projects. Every investor has their own means of doing things, and the best investors let their skills evolve as they gain confidence in their strength to spot the best deals. But regardless of great an investor becomes at recognizing deals, there are sections of the search and rehab procedure that cannot be reversed. If it is not broken, then don't try to fix it, and if you begin generating money by depending on the expertise of other people, then you must learn to take the professional advice into account.

Assessing the property

First, the investor has to become satisfied that the property can generate profit once it is rehabbed before anything else takes place. With time, most house flippers start to trust their guts when it comes to purchasing or walking away from specific properties. The more experience you get as time goes, the more refined your instincts become. But most importantly, the experience will direct you on what specifically to look out in a property that will make it a success.

Most of the properties an investor purchases to flip are sold via auctions where is no chance to look at the property over to recognize whether it is a great deal. Given that a house a flipper can make a good size of their money assessing auction properties, it is sensible to spend time building the skills required to assess properties fast. Some investors are so good at finding out what they can bid on an auction just using the pictures offered.

For those properties that an investor has the opportunity to look around and examine the deal, it is a great thing to involve a professional contractor. As a house flipper, you will become better at highlighting details that could either make or break deals, but you can never the eye of an experienced contractor. You can learn a lot by assessing properties with a contractor and pumping some cash to bring a contractor along can prevent you from making significant losses if you attempt to flip a property that may not deliver profit.

Getting the best contractor

If you want to build a career from house flipping, then you don't need a great contractor to work with you. What you need is the right contractor for you and your business. This requires a contractor that you can trust, and has the best interests in mind, is ready to work with you on flipping projects, and probably one who has several crews that can get various projects done simultaneously.

Every successful flipper has at least one contractor whom they work with often to recognize opportunities and have projects finished on time. Your contractor will know the way you want to run your business when they can take time and make decisions on your behalf, and how you are prepared to save money on the remodeling budget. It is possible to go for short cuts on a remodeling project and still attain great results; the goal is to get a contractor who is aware of building codes and materials so good that they can make replacements that receive quality results for lower prices.

Spend some time at the Home Depot

If you visit the Home Depot every weekday morning, you will see local contractors picking up supplies, purchase new equipment, and swap information with other contractors around the area. The Home Depot even simplifies the process of getting contractors by having a different loading area for contractors and their materials.

Therefore, if you are searching for a great contractor, then the Home Depot is a great place to hang out for a few weeks and watch out the contractors who often appear to purchase materials. A contractor who just comes once or twice a week is perhaps not going to be interested or even take on a flipping investor. However, those who show up every day at Home Depot are great contractors who want to take on a steady client.

Speak to other investors

It may not be easy to find trade secrets from successful house flippers, but it doesn't hurt to try. While you participate in house flipping, you will begin to meet the same people at auctions and some at distressed properties you believe you found on your own. Some of the investors could be interested in mentor new flippers while others may be tight-lipped.

Ensure that you make yourself available to other flippers around to receive referrals for great contractors. You join with professional flippers for deals and discover who you can speak to for great advice on properties. A savvy flipper may discover methods to get others to trust them and find the information they need to remain successful.

Become a member of the Real Estate Investors Association

There are plenty of reasons to take part in your local chapter of the Real Estate Investors Association (REIA), and getting the best contractor is one of them. An REIA meeting is a great place where you can start to network with different experts who can simplify your life. Contractors that want to work with house flippers often attend these meetings, and they are ready to meet you.

Regardless of where you get your contractor referrals from, you must take time to examine each referral and only do business with contractors who fulfill your guidelines. You need to recruit experienced professionals who have a reliable and mature direction to the business. After all, the type of contractor you choose to work with will have great input on the way you make decisions, and you want to be confident that you have selected the correct person to work with.

Handling your remodeling project

You get a reliable contractor to perform the remodeling projects because you need it done in the right way, but you will still require to manage the projects on your end to ensure that every project produces a profit.

Ensure you watch out on your costs and never fear to ask your contractor on the money they are spending. In case there are cost-effective means to find results, then you need to emphasize on those methods. If your contractor challenges a problem that will need more money to solve, then you should discuss all your options before making the final decision.

Have a separate contract with your contractor for each project, and there should be penalty clauses for missed deadlines. There is no problem with holding your contractor accountable for spending your money. But to ensure that your contractor defines the project deadlines. It is not good for you to set deadlines that are hard to be attained, but you can learn to agree on deadlines that are discussed with your contractor. If your contractor fails to fulfill a deadline, then you can look at the liquidated damages. This is the figure, often $100 per day, that you reduce from the final price of the project for every day it is late.

Spend part of your time to research on ways you can make improvements that add value to a home. For example, improving the technology of home and adding technological changes. You can still add value by building solar panels on a home to help reduce energy costs. In some instances, remodeling the bathroom will also generate value, but you need to know when these improvements will be effective and when they are not worth it.

Improving the appeal is one of the most critical factors in selling a property fast and for more money. You need to concentrate on landscaping and exterior changes that will draw the attention of people as they come close to the home.

The odds of landing a great flipping project and get it repaired quickly is important to your success as a house flipper. You have to spend a lot of time learning how to recognize the best deals and networking with industry experts who can assist you in making the best decisions.

Approximating repair costs on your flip

This section is focused entirely on repair and remodeling costs because of the role it plays in creating a complete price. It is hard to estimate the amount you need to offer to purchase a distressed property until you learn how much profit you can make. Both your repair and remodeling estimate is part of your general investment cost which also involves the purchase price of the property and holding costs. It is important that each flipper understand how to approximate remodeling costs, or repair costs, even if they plan to look for a contractor to estimate for them.

Why should you know how to estimate repair costs?

As your flipping business continues to grow you will discover two critical lessons:

If you decide to wait before you pull off a deal, then you are probably going to lose the deal.

Contractors work based on their schedules and don't have that time to come with you to build a comprehensive approximation.

When you don't want to estimate or make remodeling estimates on your own for your first few deals, it can affect your business. Therefore, you must try your best to learn so that your business doesn't stop because you cannot perform an estimate of repair or remodeling costs. The best deal for a distressed property may emerge on a Tuesday morning and disappear by evening. If you are relying on your contractor to perform the estimates, then you will find it hard to take advantage of the deals that you come across.

The reason for repairing and remodeling a property

Some real estate investors look for distressed properties at low prices and then flip the same properties as fast as they can. In such a business, one must learn how to deal with the highest deals if the aim is to make any substantial profit. A quick turnaround deal on the distressed property may generate in $2, 000 or $3, 0000 in profit. However, in case you remodel the property, you may see profits in the tens of thousands of dollars.

Your reputation plays a huge role when it comes to real estate investing, and having a reputation of being a high- volume distressed property buyer and seller is going to reduce your chances. Individuals who hold onto top deals often want to see something done with the property to change the neighborhood. If your goal is to purchase and sell distressed properties quickly, then you will realize that you have to create your own deals always. When you become popular as a person who utilizes distressed properties, then your phone will ring every time.

Your intention as a real estate investor is to generate profit, and the best method to make a profit is to remodel or even repair the property to ensure that it suits with the remaining completed sections in the neighborhood. Purchasing distressed property at a low price, and selling it as close to retail is the best strategy to build a successful real estate investing business.

Renovation to scale

Is it sensible to spend more money to change a property into a million-dollar showpiece in a neighborhood where the average property is estimated at $200, 000? Well, as a house flipper, you must learn to work in different areas where the value of a property comes at different levels. If you attempt to do a lot to a property, you may price it out of the market, and you may lose a lot of cash. However, losing money isn't the only way of overdoing in remodeling a house.

Your million-dollar house sitting in a $200, 000 neighborhoods may devalue the properties around it, and that may build a bad association with the homeowners in the neighborhood. At the very least, if you decide to put a highly priced property around a place with average properties, that may result in a reassessment of all the properties in that area, and thus destroy your association with other homeowners.

By overdoing it when it comes to remodeling may result in a property to stay unsold until the time you reduce the costs to avoid losing everything. People who want to purchase homes in a given neighborhood often don't want to pay more than the per house average for that particular area. Your high-priced rehab may have a difficult time to attract prospective buyers, and it may be the last project your company ever does.

The neighborhood can be your biggest friends in selling your remodeled property if you ensure that the property is in the correct price range. Homeowners hate to see abandoned properties in their neighborhoods because it hurts the property value of everyone. You could be that neighborhood's hero if you perform the correct remodeling project and change an abandoned property into a great part of the community.

Look for detail

As you work together with your contractor on setting prices on the first few rehab projects, build a checklist of things a contractor should focus and fill that list for each project. Some of the best parts of a home when it comes to remodeling estimates that people miss comprising:

The foundation

The electrical wiring Pests and insects The plumbing

The sewage system

As time goes by, you will come up with a detailed checklist that will allow you to perform your own inspections and determine the type of work that requires to be done. Your contractor will also speak in terms of costs per square feet for showing how much the work will cost. Once you look at this technique, you need to be able to apply it to your own estimates with the right degree of accuracy.

Other aspects new investors fail to consider include the title search and land survey. In many cases, any problem with the survey and the title search can be dealt with easily. However, there are times when some remodeling may fix the title or the survey, and you may need to highlight those problems and develop solutions.

Putting in the notebook

As a real estate investor, you must have two assumptions about your remodeling estimate, or the estimate you receive from the contractor, to eliminate any problem.

The project will surpass the budget

The project will take longer than expected

Although you may have the regular project that clocks in on time and on budget, you must plan for the worst situation. That is the reason why you need to add an extra of 20 percent both on the budget and the timetable. You need to include this additional percent on your own approximations and estimates you acquire from contractors. The added percent is one that you use to define the amount of money you can generate from every deal.

A great house flipper understands how to take advantage of the available resources to them, but they still know that the best deal waits for nobody. New flippers should stay clear of combining their remodeling estimates unless they have some knowledge about the general contracting. But with time, an experienced flipper should gain the correct skills required to build their own estimates and utilize the best deals when they arise.

Purchasing a distressed property

Once you have built up your network of sellers and have selected a distressed property you want to purchase, the next thing is to come up with a good offer that will win you a house. When it comes to house flipping, it is hard to get a second chance at putting an offer on the same distressed property. Thus, you must learn how to build a compelling first offer, and from there negotiate with the seller until the property becomes yours.

In most cases, the seller of distressed property is only going to sell the property as fast as possible at some profit. Wholesalers will identify the type of property they want to make, but there is always a chance for negotiation. Homeowners are always interested in selling fast than generating a massive profit, but you cannot handle homeowners the way you do with wholesalers.

For a real estate deal to succeed, all parties have to feel like they are getting the best deal. Obviously, you want to acquire property for the least price possible, but you need to know that the seller has to make a profit too. Negotiating in good faith is often going to get you further than constant aggressive negotiations.

Coming up with your initial offer

Before you choose to make an initial offer on a property, you must decide on whether the deal will work for you. You can do that by:

Deciding on the retail value of the property once you remodel by analyzing similar properties in the area. Approximate remodeling costs, liens, taxes, and holding costs.

Identify the buying price, holding costs, remodeling costs to find After Repair Value (ARV).

Remove the ARV from the retail value, and that will generate the profit you need to make.

You can avoid taking part in wrong deals by taking away 20 percent from your profit estimate to get a conservative number that you can work with. In case the numbers work on your side, then it will be time to create an offer to the homeowner.

You can change the possible profit to get either a lower or higher offer, but you cannot adjust your remodeling costs. Once you adjust the numbers and feel okay with the initial offer you have developed, then you can send the offer to the owner.

Get in touch with contingencies

When both of you and the seller reach an agreement on a given price, you should move on to put that price in writing and include plans to protect yourself. What can you do in case you don't get financing? The easiest method is to protect yourself is to involve stipulations within the contract that define the completion of the deal is contingent once:

Financing is approved A clean inspection

An agreeable appraisal

You need to also include a specific time frame for the contingencies of 30 days. If nothing takes place within 30 days of the initial agreement, then the deal is off. This will offer you the time to get all your inspections and appraisals in one place, and it is also securing you from a seller who may try to shop your price to other buyers.

Make sure that the contract defines the property as being sold "as-is" depending on the status when you agreed to the price. This will secure you from any destruction that might happen to the property and makes the owner accountable for maintaining the condition of the property in which you initially saw it.

Once you agree to a price, then you can put a deposit on the contract to ensure that the property remains there in your name. Make sure that the contingency is in the contract that requires you to get your deposit back once the deal falls through.

CHAPTER 4

Property Wholesaling

Real estate wholesaling is one of the best real estate investment methods. But for one to succeed in this business, it is important to know the little details involved in property wholesaling. So, in this section, we take you through everything that you need to know about real estate wholesaling.

But before we dive into details, you need to understand what property wholesaling means. When we talk about property wholesaling, it implies that your role is that of a middleman. You meet a motivated seller, negotiate the property for a specific low price, and then resell it for a low price but higher than the purchasing price. The differences between the two prices are your profit.

For example:

You meet an ambitious seller who wants to sell his property instantly. The first thing you need to do is to negotiate the price. It is easy to find motivated sellers because of life circumstances that they may have experienced such as foreclosure. This creates the opportunity to get the property at a much lower price. Now that you have an agreement with the property owner concerning the price move forward and allocate the property to a contract. This particular contract shall have a date by which you must get an end-buyer for the home. You begin searching for a real estate investor who is interested in purchasing investment properties for a very low price. Lastly, you close the deal with the end buyer.

Now you could be asking yourself about the money part. Well, this section comes between the negotiation with the property seller and closing the deal with the end-buyer. For instance, if you have an agreement with the seller on

$50,000 as the price of the home. Then you get a real estate investor who is ready to purchase the property for around $70, 000. The $20, 000 difference is what you pocket in from the deal. This is how you make money in real estate via wholesaling.

What is the best way to make money via real estate wholesaling?

Real estate wholesaling is one of the best methods to earn money in real estate. But the amount of money you generate depends on the size of your clients. What this means is that deciding to wholesale investment properties may be a better choice than residential properties. The reason is simple; there is always a real estate investor out there who is ready to purchase investment properties. It is simple for you to discover an end-buyer who would like to invest in property instead of living in it. Real estate investors are always searching for the best deals in the real estate sector, and in this case, you possess what they want. As a result, focusing on a specific category of clients may be a great strategy to generate money in real estate.

Well, how is real estate wholesaling different from house flipping?

Real estate property wholesaling is similar to the fix-and-flip strategy. In both methods, you acquire a property for a low price and then later resell it. Still, there are two major differences:

Fixing the property: As the name goes, it involves fixing and flipping the property. In other words, you purchase a property for a low price because of the distressed state. You make the necessary repairs and then resell it to a different person for a much higher price. This is related to forced appreciation. Once you apply the changes to the property, it increases in value so you can generate profit.

On the other hand, if you wholesale property, you don't do any repairs. You also don't purchase the property. You agree to a price and look for an end-buyer who will implement all the necessary changes.

Regardless of the direction, it doesn't imply that you will earn an extremely damaged home. In certain cases, the damages may only cost a few hundred dollars.

The return on investment: The main goal of wholesaler is to make money in real estate. When it comes to real estate investing, it is referred to as return on investment. With property wholesaling, you will be investing a few hundred dollars and your chance to acquire a high rate of return on what you have invested. But for fix and flip, you invest more time and money in remodeling the house. This doesn't imply that you don't get a great profit on your investment. It only implies that you invest a lot.

Why is property wholesaling popular?

As a real estate wholesaler, your task is to look for people interested in the property and assist the property owner in supporting the sale. Your role is not to market the property. When you adhere to these rules, you can make transactions that will not make you lose your money.

With real estate wholesaling, there is no need to put any money down, and there is nothing to lose if you cannot get an interested buyer for the home. Keep in mind that the contract expires once you fail to get a buyer. If you let a lot of contracts to expire, then your track record is ruined. However, if you work extremely hard and study the business, you can become a great expert at uniting buyers and sellers in the low-risk business.

Basic concepts of wholesaling

This section will focus on the basic elements you must have before you can start wholesaling properties. That includes:

Approaching the seller- There is a correct way and wrong way to introduce your services and yourself to a property owner.

Math and Negotiations-You must be good working with numbers in wholesaling, and you need to understand how to use the same numbers to come up with the best deal.

Get in touch with the owner of Property-There are various ways to create wholesaling contracts that you must know.

Presenting the Deal-You will learn the best ways to land lucrative deals and the way to present your real estate deal.

Legality

You have made the first step towards real estate property wholesaling by reading this chapter. Now is time to dive deep into the world of wholesaling and demonstrate to you how you can get started.

For you to expand your network of sellers with your real estate wholesaling business, you must look for methods to reach out to people who may be interested in your services. As long as you regularly update your details, respond to your metrics, and continue to collect new information, you will find the sellers to speak to.

There are different methods you can use to market your business services to a specific audience, but one of the most effective methods is direct mail marketing. This particular marketing requires generation and mailing of physical flyers and data sheets to possible sellers to develop an interest in your business.

Why is direct mail the best?

There are a few reasons as to why successful property wholesalers prefer direct mail. First, a wholesaler who regularly updates their direct mail contact will build a list that contains names of people who want to sell their homes. Direct mail eliminates the guess away from marketing and allows you to talk directly to your audience.

It can be quite difficult for individuals who depend on technology to understand the power of paper. When a buyer visits a property you want to sell holding your flyer on their hands, then you can recognize how powerful direct mail can be. A marketing piece relays a single message, and on a piece of paper. This message is not diluted with pop-up ads and thousands of other irrelevant digital marketing.

Tips to creating a great direct mail campaign

Design your flyers

Each mail should feature a single message, and that message should be clearly defined in the entire flyer. For instance, if you are searching for new sellers, then your message should introduce your services to distressed property owners. On the flyer, you need to avoid putting every detail about other properties that you are selling, or anything that can interfere with your message.

Call to Action (CTA)

Each marketing piece you develop should finish with a call to action. The CTA should summarize the message in your flyer and encourage your readers to take action. For example, the flyer describing who you are to prospective sellers can finish with a CTA that says:

Get in touch with me today by phone or email to learn more about how I can assist you in selling your home fast.

By the time the reader comes to read your CTA, they shall have all the information they need to make a decision. The CTA encourages readers to act on that decision instantly and take whichever action you want them to do.

Developing mailing lists

Building a list of prospective real estate sellers are going to require a lot of energy and time to update regularly. It is often a great idea to separate seller lists depending on the place where you got the information to simplify the process of updating lists regularly. You can build lists of possible sellers by:

Getting in touch with local banks to discuss getting lists of properties either in foreclosure or close to attaining a foreclosure. You will be shocked at the number of banks ready to offer this information.

Look online for any listings of vacant properties to see whether the owners are interested in selling the properties.

Reading published lists of bankruptcies in the local newspaper.

They are making use of lists in the newspaper titles "Recent Notice of Default" that will indicate the kind of property that owners want to sell because they are delaying on their mortgages.

Invest in real estate software that will personalize the searches online for homes with a specific amount of equity. Sometimes, people who have a lot of equity in their homes may want to sell homes quickly and gather their equity.

Visit your local city hall to look for lists of property owners who live out-of-state and who are interested in selling their local properties.

Get in touch with the local fire department to ask whether you can be given a list of properties recently destroyed by fire. You can still follow the local fire and police calls in the newspaper every day to get addresses of destroyed properties.

List brokers

The internet has a lot of companies that are ready to create custom real estate property lists depending on your criteria.

Creating an effective campaign

Your direct mail skills always evolve as you learn more about how the process work, and the process that doesn't work. For instance, try to apply a handwritten-looking font on one type of mailer and then a decent font on the other. Monitor the responses you receive and take advantage of the strategy that gets a lot of responses.

Your direct email piece will compete directly with other real estate wholesalers, which is the reason why you need to monitor each result for every mailer and learn from the good and bad responses. Maybe you discover that a handwritten-looking envelope integrated with a professional looking direct mail letter is the right mix to get results. Each moment you learn something from your previous direct mail campaigns, you must use that information to make the next one better.

The message

What type of message works best with each audience? You may realize that people who possess abandoned homes respond better to professional looking messages, while those nearing a foreclosure prefer an informal approach. You need to note down these observations and apply them to build messages that work well for every audience.

Costs

It is important that you are always on the lookout for methods to ensure your direct mailing costs stay low. Monitor your track costs and ensure that you compare your costs to your tenants. You can still reduce your costs by regularly updating your lists and searching bulk mail discounts.

If you purchase from list brokers, then it is important to monitor the results you get with the lists and avoid using brokers that will send you bad addresses. You may also want to ensure that your lists receive responses that generate revenue to avoid wasting money on the future lists.

MailMerge And Custom Mailings

MailMerge is a program that works directly with the Microsoft Excel application to assist in building custom envelopes and letters for each contact you have. With the MailMerge, you can create fields from Excel and complete in your letter and envelope templates using custom information. Below is how MailMerge operates:

Outsourcing

You can always outsource your direct mail campaigns to an experienced organization that is focused on these types of marketing tactics. With a great outsourcing company, you can free yourself and get more sellers to expand your inventory.

Direct mail is a great marketing tool for any type of real estate wholesaler. Once your lists are updated correctly, and you continue to run experiments until you discover the correct message for every audience, you will begin to find the resources you require to build your business.

Driving for dollars is one of the real estate wholesaler marketing strategies that require the discovery of properties that may not appear on any list compiled. There are numerous methods to apply the drive for dollars' strategy, and you will finally build your own method depending on your experience. Some wholesalers prefer to apply the driving for dollars' campaign over compiling lists from online research. However, successful wholesalers understand that they must use each available strategy to get properties to represent.

This section will show you on the process of assessing properties and adding them to your potential list. Driving for dollars is a strategy of looking for properties in your neighborhood while driving. It is as simple as getting into your car and, starting to scour properties near your neighborhood. While it appears simple, there is a lot of preparation that you need to do before you go hunting.

This strategy is still your opportunity to interact with the residents of your neighborhoods and introduce yourself. This is the point where you employ your negotiation skills and professional presentation skills. The friendlier and approachable you become, the more information you gain from residents concerning a distressed property. Driving for dollars will not only allow you to add properties to your inventory, but it will also assist you to increase your referral network.

How to get started with driving for dollars

As with any plan for marketing in real estate, the driving for the dollar isn't something that you should wake up and decide to do. It is critical that you spend time to compile a list and highlight neighborhoods that you want to drive through before you get into the field. You can decide to select your own method for determining the type of neighborhoods to visit. Here are some ideas for you:

The average age of homes. Possible equity in the homes

Crime percent rate. A lower crime percent makes it easier to sell properties to house flippers.

The challenge with driving for dollars without a strategy is that you don't have a hint of what type of properties you are looking for. Keep in mind that time is valuable, and you want to ensure that you optimize your return anytime you are marketing.

Things that you should have

As you prepare to go driving, you should look for the following things:

A camera

Your business cards to give to your neighborhood.

Flies that describe your business to provide your neighborhood people. Your lists

Tips for finding the best moments to drive for dollars

When you focus on a specific neighborhood for dollars, any property near that neighborhood is a good game. However, there are some clues that you must look for to show that a property is distressed, or the owners are going through certain problems that may result in a distressed property in the coming future.

Here are the best tips to use to locate possible properties while driving for dollars:

Properties that don't have an outdoor decoration for Christmas, or interior decorations seen via the windows. This may show a religious preference, but it can also be a great sign of a distressed property.

Properties that have developed newspapers on the porch that are cleaned once or twice a month. Properties with garbage collection in different places.

Properties featuring boarded up doors, or windows. Properties without lights on at night.

Properties attached with ordinance notice at the front doors.

Let dive into the process

It can take a few drives through a neighborhood before you make up your mind to drive for dollars. For example, it can take several weeks of constant driving through a neighborhood to select the properties that don't put their garbage out on collection day. However, once you gather all the information necessary, it is time to go driving through for dollars.

While you drive through the neighborhood, you will use your camera to take pictures of properties you think may be prospective inventory items. Look for clear pictures of the worst features of the properties so that you can create accurate notes when you return to your office. Make use of the pen and paper to take note of the addresses you snapped pictures, and make notes on the status of the properties and neighborhood in general.

What you will be looking for

You will be searching for a distressed property that has out-of-state owners or is owner-occupied. These describe properties which you can market your services to the owners and receive immediate feedback. An abandoned property owned by banks needs a completely different process for buying. You need to separate the bank owned properties and concentrate on the properties that you can contact.

You can look for owners of these properties via your county's Central Appraisal District (CAD). Your local CAD is easy to get by using Google. The CAD will show you who possesses the property, and it will further provide you with the contact information for out-of-state owners as well. You can use your smartphone to connect with the CAD while you are in the field to avoid wasting time to process bank-owned properties, or you can confirm the CAD when you reach to the office and separate the bank-owned properties from the rest.

Processing your information

The information you gather while driving for dollars can be inserted on a spreadsheet that is different from the rest of your information to ensure that marketing is simple. Once you get a property to add to your possible pool, you must record the way you found that property so that you can send the correct type of marketing piece to the property owner.

When you go back to your office, you will take all the addresses you have gathered and begin to create an owner contact list depending on your findings. Make sure you attach your photos to each list entry to notify yourself of why you placed that property on your list in the first place.

Of course, abandoned properties are clear as to why they are distressed, but the owner-occupied properties you come across is going to be a bit difficult to classify. You aim to generate a thousand dollars from properties that aren't on any pre-foreclosure list you have created. Driving for dollars prevents these properties from being picked by others, but you may have to apply a customized marketing piece to speak to homeowners who currently occupy distressed homes effectively.

While you drive for dollars, you may be asked by the residents who are a bit curious to know why you are doing it. These are people whom you can speak to about relaying your information on other distressed properties in the area, or they may own a distressed property of their own. Driving for dollars involves the way you will reach out to communities where you work and build good relationships with the local people.

Some advice on the best approach

If you begin knocking on the doors of distressed property owners, then you may experience solicitation challenges. Besides, your purpose of looking for dollars is to find properties to add to your list. Therefore, knocking on the doors can slow down your efforts rather than optimize your results.

When a distressed property is owned by a landlord and occupied by tenants, then you may not want to attempt to leave any information with the tenants. Your target should be on the property owners and not anyone else. You may even get into trouble for leaving a real estate wholesaling with a tenant who has no idea that their property is distressed.

The correct approach to optimize the driving for dollars' campaign is to develop a plan and realize exactly what you are searching for when you are in the field. Driving for dollars involves finding properties that do not appear on any of your lists, and that it will assist you to be a step ahead of the competition.

When you decide that wholesaling is the thing that you want to do in your career, you must instantly drive yourself into what you do if you want to realize success. The more people you speak to, and the more familiar you become with the location you are working in, the information you will have to expand your business. Once you have a detailed knowledge of your territory and the way things operate within that territory, then you will be boosting yourself on the competition.

Few activities in marketing assist you to discover everything you want to know concerning the geographic location you are working in such as door knocking. When you take advantage of door knocking to make yourself known to the people in the area where you work, you tend to allow yourself to build a strong bond with the community that can result in a never-ending source of property referrals. There is a lot to door knocking than just moving from one property to the next and introducing yourself. Once you discover how to optimize the door knocking strategy, you will start to see why many successful wholesalers use it often.

Door knocking. What is it?

As the name goes, you move from door to door and introduce yourself to property owners in a specific neighborhood. You are directed by a list of potential sellers created from your research. You can take the door knocking one street at a time, or you can decide to be ambitious and attempt to cover the whole neighborhood at once. For you to become effective, it is important to knock on a door twice a year to confirm that your name and business remain as fresh as possible in the minds of people.

Why should you go back to door knocking?

Many people who live in neighborhoods dislike seeing abandoned properties reduce the property values and result in criminals living in the area. Door knocking is an excellent method to discover the type of properties in an abandoned area.

Searching for distressed properties that don't appear like distressed

Sometimes it is hard to tell a book by its cover, and each wholesaler in the area may be walking by a distressed house and not even realize. You may knock on the door of the beautiful looking property and learn that the owner is three months behind paying their mortgage and wants to sell it quickly. You will know this because you came across an address while researching on pre-foreclosures with different banks.

Create a referral network

Many wholesalers use door knocking with the main purpose of building a large referral network with the local people. For instance, you can develop a flyer that promises to pay each resident with $100 for each property they direct your way that you finally get a buyer. It will cost you zero to set up a massive referral network with residents, but it can generate a stream of great property referrals. Regardless of the type of list your prospective generates, they can all become an important part of your network that generates more leads to your business.

Develop a reputation as that kind of person who can assist homeowners

Building a good reputation among distressed property owners in a place where you want to sell properties is highly going to support your business. As you go knocking doors of property owners and explain to people the way you can assist distressed homeowners, you will learn that people in these neighborhoods go beyond their abilities to suggest to you homeowners who may need your services.

Develop a system

Door knocking is something that you will want to make it a regular part of your business marketing strategy. You will conduct a lot of marketing for your wholesaling business, but few marketing techniques provide you with benefits than door knocking. When you build a list of prospective, then purpose to get into the neighborhoods and see those properties. Your door knocking procedures should be directed by the lists you build from the many hours of research. Time is important in real estate wholesaling, and the earlier you introduce yourself to distressed property owners, the earlier you can make money by assisting them in selling their properties.

The odds that you will end a deal to represent a property while knocking on the door depends on the quality of your list. However, the more doors you knock, the larger your referral network grows, and the more goodwill you will develop all of the homeowners in your local area. It may take time for the door knocking to pay off, but when it does pay, it can be the most successful forms of marketing you will ever do.

Bandit signs/ yard signs

Also known as yard signs, these are signs where you post near towns in places that can be easily seen. You can post them in the property yards you are currently listing, real estate attorneys, title insurance companies, and any other form of business that handles real estate transactions. The most critical thing is to ensure that you put your yard signs in places where many people will see them. Yard signs are affordable and easy to install.

Bandit signs are posted on telephone poles and any place that they can be seen by traffic. Typically, you want to post them at intersections and junctions where traffic stops so that people can read the signs. There are different ways of making bandit signs, and it is vital that you research well to know the types of signs that are effective in specific areas of your area.

Placing signs

There are still other great places where you can place the signs. The walls outside popular sports stadiums and light poles are excellent areas to put your signs because people tend to spend most of their time waiting in line, or preparing for the game. The same is true for popular nightclubs around your city.

If you get permission to post signs in parking ramps, then you will have a captive audience daily that will be reading your signs. Public parks can as well be great places for signs because many people visit the park and they have enough time to read a sign that draws their attention. In places where you are sure people will gather, you should make an effort to get your signs into visible places.

The advantage of the yard and bandit signs

Both yard and bandit signs are cheap and easy to acquire. There are different vendors online that offer excellent work for a low price. They capture the attention, and you will have a good percentage of people who will read the signs if you place them in the correct places.

Great signs will push your brand and get people to identify your company name on sight. Signs also draw the attention of buyers, investors, and sellers to help you develop your database of contacts.

The drawbacks of the yard and bandit signs

Some communities have banned these signs, which could mean more trouble if you use them. Your yard signs posted on public property could result in police and asked to pay fines. Bandit signs removed from telephone lines could lead to serious legal effects for you that will worsen in case you are marked as a repeat offender.

Some wholesalers look at fines as the cost of doing business because their yard and bandit signs generate a continuous stream of a lucrative business. However, it might reach the point where you are handling more than a few fines because of the constant signs.

What you should know before getting into real estate property wholesaling

It takes the right individual to be in the right place for success. As a result, before you can get into real estate wholesaling, take time to decide whether wholesaling will work for you in the real estate sector. Now, this is not a move to sweet talk you out of it, but a word of encouragement to you that you assess the situation first and decide whether you want to do it or not. For you to wholesale real estate properties, you need to have the correct real estate knowledge and education. You also need to have the right connections and the correct negotiation skills. These are important factors in real estate wholesaling.

Additionally, you need to consider the pros and cons of real estate wholesaling. Although wholesaling is the best solution to the question, "How to make money in real estate?", the challenge is that it's not guaranteed. What this really means is that if you fail to get a property buyer, you would have wasted a lot of time. This is the same reason why you must have connections when using these investment strategies. Networks simplify the process of getting clients, your case; they are called buyers.

One of the main things of wholesaling investment properties is learning the housing market. Real estate wholesaling can be one of the quickest means to learn more about the real estate market. As a result, diving into it will provide you with a great experience improvement.

Lastly, real estate wholesaling is a great thing as long as you are aware of what you are getting into. But this doesn't mean that you cannot involve other profitable investment methods. It only means that you need to take into account the shortcomings and find a way forward.

CHAPTER 5

Real Estate Investment Deals

When it comes to investment properties, the most commonly asked question is where a person can get funding for the next deal.

If you are thinking of purchasing a house for investment, but you don't have sufficient money in your bank account, don't worry. Fortunately, there are many financing opportunities than you know. Picking the right choice for your investment strategy and specific instance save you a huge amount of money.

In this section, you will learn about the various loans available for financing your next real estate investment.

1. Conventional loans

This is one of the most common types of mortgage. In a conventional loan, you pay a certain amount of money before the bank provides you with the remaining money. Although a lot of banks let borrowers pay as little as 5% of the buying price, investors have no option but put down more than that. As such, many investors pay a down payment of 20%, so that the loan is not considered as part of the private mortgage insurance. (PMI).

Advantages

Easy to understand

The most common type of financing, so it is easy to shop around for the best terms and rates. Conventional loans are one of the lowest interest rates for any loan options.

Disadvantages

Conventional loans have a limit.

You require to have a credit score of more than 640 to qualify.

It is a bit difficult to qualify if you purchase properties using LLC instead of putting them in your name.

2. Veteran Affairs (VA) loan

Getting a VA loan is a great achievement of working in the military. This loan provides no-down-payment loans to veterans, chosen military spouses, and service members. Same to FHA loan, you will have to stay in the home for a minimum of one year. One good thing with this type of loan is that you can purchase as many houses as you would like as long as you don't surpass the set amount, and you stay in each one for a minimum of one year. The limiting aspect isn't the number of houses; it is the amount you are awarded.

Advantages

PMI not needed for VA loans. It has the lowest interest rate.

No down payment. Very low closing costs. With the VA loans, the seller will have to pay for some of the closings costs the buyer would always pay.

A high ratio of debt-to-income allowed.

You can correctly develop a portfolio of rental properties without any down payment by living in every house for a year, or renting out each and moving on.

Disadvantages

Not available to everyone.

You will need to live in the property for at least one year. A lot of paperwork at the time of settlement.

There is a specific VA funding charge that is included in your loan that the VA asks to ensure the program continues to run.

3. 203(k) loan

The 203(k) loan resembles the FHA loan because it is centered a lot toward homeowners than investors. This is an owner-occupied, 3.5% down payment loan that lets you lump the rehab costs into the mortgage.

Advantages

You can support the entire project with one lender.

You can expand the choices to include distressed and foreclosed homes.

You can request a better deal on a property that deserves rehab, which means you can gain immediate equity.

If you do the rehab work yourself, you can move on to discuss the costs below the retail process.

No need to look for additional money for rehab costs, and when you are done, the home will possibly be worth more than the loan amount.

Disadvantages

Contractors have to be voted and approved by your lender.

Only accessible to owner-occupants- you must live at the property as your main residence. In general, the amount of paperwork is more during and after settlement.

4. Private money

This one refers to finances from individual investors. There are no institutions involved here. In this method, you can ask for support from family, co-workers, or a few close friends you have interacted with at your local real estate investing groups. In general, private money will be costlier than a traditional mortgage. However, the terms set are more flexible. Additionally, the requirements to qualify for this type of funding is friendly.

Pros

Cons

Minimum qualifications are demanded. Has a simple and flexible structure.

Has a higher interest rate than other loans.

You may need to look for an attorney to create a financial contract. The terms are shorter (3-5) years.

In case things don't go well, it may destroy the relationship between you and the lender.

5. Hard money

This resembles private money; the only difference is that the money doesn't come from an individual but a hard- money lender. For this type of loan, the lender uses a hard asset to protect the loan. Hard money is a form of short- term loan used by borrowers to purchase fix up and flip. In general, you can get hard money to account for 70-80% of the property bought before rehab. Just like private money, hard-money lenders cut a huge interest and include other charges such as origination fees.

Pros

Cons

It is easy to get because the loan is protected by property. Has a simple and flexible loan structure.

Lenders of hard money know the special needs of real estate investors and provide quick loan funding and approval.

The rate of interest is higher than other loans.

It can be quite expensive if a person is thought to be risky.

There are many methods to employ to finance your real estate investment deals. Understanding everything about each method is crucial. It is important that you consider all the available options rather than jump into traditional methods of financing. Find time to discuss your methods and choices with a professional loan officer who has interacted with investors and develop the best financing plan for your situations, knowing that those situations change over time.

The world has people who are looking for great places to invest their money. Therefore, if you have a good record of generating profit with your real estate investment, then getting a financing option will not be a big problem for you. You may need to become a bit creative.

Find the best deals and the investing strategies

People continue to join real estate to generate wealth, and the more people want to purchase real estate properties, the harder it becomes to find deals. It is that simple as supply and demand in business.

As a result, the method that investors employed to find deals in the past is quickly changing. Unlike a few years ago where it was possible to get a deal using MLS, today is almost impossible. But instead, smart investors are redefining their methods of finding deals. At the end of the day, if you want something that no one else can get, it is a must that you do something that no one else will do to earn.

So, are you ready to learn what to do what everyone is not doing? If yes, here are a few methods that you can apply to strike a great deal.

Let's start!

1. Try to purchase foreclosed properties from a bank.

When a person fails to pay his or her mortgage for a certain period, the lender will decide to repossess the property and chase away the occupants. Once the house is empty, the lender goes on to list the house for sale on the market, by using a local real estate channel.

While the foreclosure is a sad thing, these homes can be one of the best deals you can come across in real estate. Banks will always want to remain in the business of lending money, and not maintaining homes or houses, so they are always quick to provide massive discounts just to remove the deal from their records. But though these are one of the best deals ever, you can only strike a great deal on foreclosed properties, if you know the methods of purchasing foreclosures.

Since the foreclosure process requires different years; these properties require serious updating and repair. In this case, more discounts may be generated to compensate the buyers.

2. Make sure you are the first or the last.

In real estate business, the early bird always catches the worm. Sometimes, it is not the highest offer for a property that is accepted; it's but the first. As a result, if you are searching for a great deal, you must be quick to snatch it. Look for pre-approval from a bank so that you can jump at any property anytime, and let your real estate agent set you up to receive automatic email alerts reminding you of new property that comes to the market.

Next, don't wait for anything but check it out immediately, and send an offer the same day if you can.

Alternatively, you can also find the best deals by looking at properties that have been in the market for a long time. The owners of these properties are usually ready to sell for a discount because they are tired of holding on to the same property. In most cases, they may have been making two mortgage payments and will accept any offer.

3. Look for absent property owners privately.

In a competitive real estate, great deals can be very difficult to find because of the huge number of people hunting for a house. In some places, a single home for sale may receive more than a dozen offers in the first few days.

As a result, the best trick real estate investors employ today to get in touch with contact owners and ask them to sell. At any moment, a great percentage of the population will listen to this option, so why should you not reach out to them before they list it with a real estate agent?

The best people to focus on is absentee owners; these are individuals who own a given property but don't live there. They could be landlord or owners who have inherited their houses and are not sure what to do with them. You can get these deals in different ways, such as:

Purchasing public record list.

Searching for houses that appear vacant.

Making a call to mom-and-pop landlords who have listed properties "for rent" on the Craigslist. Tell them that you are not interested in renting the property, but you would like to speak with them about purchasing.

4. Eviction records

Evictions aren't a good thing. It is messy, time-intensive, and costly. During the time of eviction, many landlords start to ask questions about why they are involved in this game.

This is the reason why focusing on landlords who are in the process of an eviction can be so good. They are experiencing a problem, and there is a good chance they will be happy to get out of the property quickly.

Well, how can you target these landlords?

Evictions are an aspect of public record in many counties of America. This means that you can visit your local county administration office and request to see a list of the current evictions happening. Various counties and states conduct evictions in different ways, but if you ask it shouldn't be difficult to find.

5. Direct mail

Lastly, you must recognize that finding the best deals is possibly a 'numbers game.' So if you have a list of people who can be your potential sellers, you can decide to send them letters, having the belief that a small percentage may call you to discuss, and a few of those may end up selling you their properties.

Although this may look cheap on the surface, direct email marketers know that the proof lies in the percentages. Lastly, if you remain passionate about your goal to find sellers, then you will possibly find many. One thing that you must know is that people are always ready to help you accomplish your goals, you need to let the world know what you want, and the rest will help you get it.

How to analyze deals and make offers?

As a real estate investor, you can either build or destroy your investment when you pay a lot for a property; you may end up losing all your shorts. Find a great deal on a home, and it may make a big difference.

Some programs exist that promise you to get deals from the comfort of your home. As long as you have a stable internet connection, a computer, and a telephone you are in business. But remember when the deal is so good, think twice. The truth is that there is a lot that is done apart from playing around with numbers.

While feelings can dictate whether you will buy a property or not, there is a lot more than just your feelings. Typically, you want a real estate deal that will fulfill your goals. To realize that, you must know how to analyze and value the property, including predicting whether it's going to generate money.

Your responsibility as you assess various properties is to ignore the list of prices, or what the sellers might want and concentrate on what is important to you.

Don't be scared about the property assessment of the city or whether the sellers paid for it. Those numbers aren't that important. You might use them while negotiating if it comes to that point, but for the sake of analyzing the property, they are not necessary.

As you assess the property, pay attention to the following things:

What is the place zoned out for? What else can you add there? Can you create an office space or more units?

Are there any regulations or rules set on the use of the property? What are the forms of transport near the property?

What status is the property in?

Are there any problems caused by the environment near the property? This can be bed bugs, earthquakes, termites, mold and many more.

Who are the occupants? Owners of the property or tenants?

What else is in the area that is attractive for someone living there? Does it have parks?

What is your gut telling you when you set eyes on the property? How is the experience when you are in the property?

Some of the things mentioned here you can check using google maps and gather other information from the internet. However, many of these questions require that you show up physically in the property to answer them accurately.

Next, to determine the values, you will require to run the same analysis on other properties that are on the market, including the ones that have been sold recently in the area. You will also need to look for time to calculate the rent rate you can earn for the property.

In case you find two properties with the same size and location, but one is more expensive than the other, it is your task to find out why. Remember, the cheaper property could be in a worse location. Or it could be in a noisy street, or close to a garbage dump where it receives less sunlight. These are just a few of the many things that you will have to figure out.

Things you need to analyze a real estate deal and compute the cash flow

You will require to collect most of the following information to determine the cash flow:

Property taxes. Property maintenance Recycling/garbage fee Rent

Electricity Heat

Aside from this, you will need to develop a rough idea of how much you will require to pay as a down payment. Most of the items listed above can be estimated until you receive an accepted offer on the property, at which point you will have an easy route to the real numbers. But the more actual numbers you get from the seller and your different sources, the more accurate your cash flow prediction will be.

Ways to determine whether a property is a great real estate deal

Every property buyer wants a great deal while buying a real estate. Although the price is important, finding a property that can be destroyed with the least effort and time cannot be that easy. Anyone who buys a house with the purpose to fix it up to understands that there could be hidden challenges that arise without warning and aren't easy to identify, even if you have the best home assessment. The ability to tell whether a house is worth its investment requires a keen eye. Here are tips that you can use to tell whether a property can be a great deal.

1. Determine zoning problems and liens

In general, one way that you can know is when a property has a complication that may result in automatic "no" for most investors. Zoning problems and liens on a little non-institutional grade property are the best spots.

2. Stick to the 1% rule

There are different methods to review an investment return when purchasing an income property. As a rule of thumb, clients are advised to use the 1% rule that demands the income property should rent for around 1% of the buying price to generate positive cash flow.

3. Review the CAP Rate

Cap rate is one great signal, although there are some sensible reasons for a few sellers to become motivated than others. Also, the price per square foot or the price per door vs. neighborhood comps as good metrics if used well.

4. Look at the roofline

This can help you to see if the house appears sturdy, simple, elegant, vulnerable, or weak.

5. Develop a sense of condition and presentation

The status of the property plus how it has been presented will determine whether the property can be bought at a discount. So in case, the property doesn't have an online photo, then it probably has a zero-curb appeal. It also implies that a substantial discount can be asked on the buying price and the listing agent doesn't have a lot of work to do, and may just after a quick sale.

CHAPTER 6

Secrets of successful real estate investors

S ince 2008, real estate investment has made most American accumulate lots of money. Based on a report by Morgan Stanley, around 77% of millionaire's have an investment in real estate. Do you want to join this group of rich men and women? Are you wondering what their secret could be? Fortunately, generating money with real estate is not a miracle

1. Make the necessary plan first

Starting real estate without a plan isn't the right thing to do. Before you dive in, define specific goals and objectives.

First, develop your plan. Next, you look for a house to suit that plan. Select your investment model, and then start to look for homes to match that. Don't look for a strategy once you find the property.

2. Become serious with agreements

Remember that contracts are a critical plus the agreement of buying and selling a property for a home. Contracts have a clear request including the consequence, time, and terms. You need to make sure that you completely understand all the requirements before you sign.

3. Remove your calculator

According to a real estate expert Scott McGillivray, numbers are vital in this business. Once you invest in a property, you must learn to enjoy performing different calculations. Don't be too focused on the house.

4. Buyer Beware

Real estate agents possess their own code. So you must be smart and learn to read between the line when scanning through listings.

5. Treat your real estate investment like a business

To achieve the success, you must work at it. You must become an active landlord, and monitor everything that is happening with your rental properties. Stay ahead of maintenance and repairs. Maintain great records. Don't look for shortcuts but follow the rules. If you can treat your real estate business with the required attention, you are likely to make the right decisions based on facts and numbers, instead of emotions.

6. Prepare for a long-term commitment

Don't be deceived by the get-rich schemes. Real estate is a long-term investment despite its state of illiquidity. It requires hard work, commitment and time. You will not get rich overnight, but when you do it right, real estate generates a good profit on investment.

7. Continue learning

The people who have made it in real estate know that there is always something to learn. As a result, many of them spend countless hours reading books, listings, or anything that they can get their hands on. Once they possess properties, they are faced with new types of challenges. Fortunately, many of them have experienced those challenges, and by reading useful real estate material, one can know how to handle a given problem. However, you can never find an answer to a problem if you stop researching and reading helpful material. Therefore, make sure that you never stop learning.

8. Now get out from your comfort zone

You will never make money in real estate if you decide to sit in one place every day. You must get out and start to research. You must be willing to meet your fellow investors and landlords. Walk through properties. Send different offers, even low ones. A real estate kingdom isn't built in a single day. It can take months to find the correct property at the right place. However, you will never find it if you don't research homes and scan through possible investments. So jump in!

9. Ask for help

Learning the tricks of succeeding in real estate is quite difficult for someone who wants to do things on their own. The best real estate investors attribute a fraction of their success to others. These can be lawyers, mentors, or any supportive friend. Instead of risking your time and money to solve a complex problem, you can also employ the expertise of other people.

10. Develop a network

A network is key in supporting and creating opportunities for both experienced and new real estate investors. This group should consist of a mentor, members of a non-profit organization, business partners and clients. Since most of the real estate investing depend on experimental learning, smart real estate investors know they need to build a network.

CONCLUSION

U p until this point we have looked at many different topics in real estate investment. As such, we believe that you know how to find the best investment properties in real estate, you have understood the concept of house flipping, property wholesaling, how to identify the best real estate investment deals and many more.

So.... what next?

The next step is to take a realistic review of yourself. Ask yourself the following questions:

1. Why do I want to invest in real estate? Are you getting into real estate just because you got laid off or you want to protect your retirement plan? How you respond to this question will set the tone for how you do everything else.

2. What are your skills, knowledge, and abilities in real estate?

3. What is your financial strength? This is important because if you don't have the funds or access to funds, your choices will be less.

4. How much time can you commit to real estate investing? If you are working on a full-time job and have a family. You will have to be fair to yourself. Don't deceive yourself that you are going to work an extra 30 hours a week on real estate. You will only discourage yourself.

5. Do you have a plan, even a general plan that describes where you want to be in your real estate business say in a year, three years, etc.? This is also necessary because as you gain more experience more opportunities emerge.

6. What are some of the non-financial resources available?

While there are other questions that you need to ask yourself, the success of your real estate business will revolve around the time and response to the above questions. Spending time to "get it right" at the start will prevent many challenges that may arise down the road.

CPSIA information can be obtained
at www.ICGtesting.com
Printed in the USA
LVHW010355100221
678895LV00004B/844